Discovering Women in Polish Design:

Interviews & Conversations

Gian Luca Amadei

Adam Mickiewicz Institute
CULTURE.PL

POLSKA! YEAR

Patron HM The Queen
Patron HE The President
of the Republic of Poland

The book is a result of study visits organised by
the Adam Mickiewicz Institute in preparation for
POLSKA! YEAR

Discovering Women in Polish Design:
Interviews & Conversations
www.womenindesign.pl

Copyright by Adam Mickiewicz Institute
Copyright by Anna Pietrzyk-Simone
Copyright by Gian Luca Amadei

Publisher / Adam Mickiewicz Institute, ul. Mokotowska 25, 00-560 Warszawa

Author & book concept / Gian Luca Amadei
Managing editor & promotion / Anna Pietrzyk–Simone
Coordination / Anna Mroczkowska (POLSKA! YEAR Team)
Photography / Dario Lombardi
Designer / Kieran Gardner
Sub-editor / Gwen Webber
Advert & website design / Monika Zawadzka

ISBN 978-83-60263-86-8

Warsaw 2009

Discovering Women in Polish Design:

Interviews & Conversations

by Gian Luca Amadei
portraits by Dario Lombardi

Acknowledgments

) Many people have helped in the development of this book.

Anna Mroczkowska (POLSKA! YEAR Team) for her coordination of our trips to Poland and meetings in London. The team at the Adam Mickiewicz Institute for the trust they have put in this project.

Vicky Richardson, editor of Blueprint, who believed in this project since its inception giving me strength and precious advice during its development and contributing to the book with her foreword.

The Polish Cultural Institute in London for its support and availability.

Czesława Frejlich, Anna Maga and Anna Frąckiewicz for their extraordinary contribution to the book.

Monika Zawadzka for the website and advert design.

Stacey Hunter and Emma Halliday, who have generously shared their knowledge and expertise in running book projects.

Tim Ellis for his patience and remarkable help in defining the final concept for the book cover.

Sean Simone who has been a strong support and for kindly reading the first draft of the book.

3F Studio in Warsaw for making their showroom available for interviews.

Jocelyn Bailey for her amazing patience in transcribing the interviews from the original recordings.

All of the designers interviewed for the project.

And finally to the team that worked on this book (in alphabetical order): Kieran Gardner, Dario Lombardi, Anna Pietrzyk-Simone and Gwen Webber. We have not all been in the same place at any one time, yet we all shared the love and passion for this project.

Contents

FOREWORD
Vicky Richardson
Editor — Blueprint

) Given that design is a human-centred activity, it's surprising that design publications are usually filled with lifeless images of inanimate objects. This book is very different. It tells stories of what life is like as a designer, and reveals some of the commitment and dedication that is required to make good work. In many ways the lives of the interview subjects resonate with designers' experiences across the world. But this book is also very specific, focusing on the experience of women working in design in Poland, and in the process provides an insight into one of the most fast-changing societies in Europe.

It's often the case that an outsider can grasp a situation more clearly than someone in the thick of things: hence we find the author of this book Gian Luca Amadei – an Italian male living in the UK – writing a book about Polish female designers.

I have worked with Luca for nearly five years at Blueprint, where he is the magazine's product editor. One of Luca's particular talents is being able to see things with fresh eyes and tremendous enthusiasm, often drawing out experiences and ideas that others have overlooked.

When Luca travelled to Warsaw for a three-day study trip in October 2007 he was struck by the fact that of the 15 or so designers he met only about three of them were men. He was also intrigued to find that some of those women, who were either practicing designers, directors of design institutes, or writers, had no academic or formal training in design, but all had found their way into it through their passion for the subject.

The interviews he conducted with designers during 2008 and 2009 are remarkable. Along with the sensitive portraits taken by Italian photographer Dario Lombardi, they show designers as ordinary working people, their hopes and their struggles to build careers and get their work produced. We learn about their relationships with manufacturers, and the interesting history of production in Poland, which once was one of the biggest export economies in the world. But while Poland's manufacturers have long worked with designers, through and for other companies around Europe, they have only recently begun to develop relationships with home-grown designers.

The timing of this book could not be better. Its publication during the London Design Festival is also at the midpoint of POLSKA! YEAR, a festival of Polish culture in the UK, running from May 2009 to May 2010. Many of the women whose lives and careers you'll discover in the book, have a strong desire for change. Some make polemical points about the exploitation of designers; about the lack of practical expertise within design education, and there are also examples of women making progress in these arenas. This excellent book should give strength to designers in Poland and around the world that the challenges they face are not unique, and that change is possible against the odds.

PREFACE
Gian Luca Amadei

) **Visiting Poland for the first time in** October 2007, I had an insight into a design community I didn't know even existed. It was yet more refreshing to discover that the Polish design scene has a remarkable number of women designers.

Immensely influential on the direction of Polish design, this female-dominated industry is partly attributed to the education system. In Polish universities, designers gain a fine arts education, which attracts more women to study than it does men. Whether product designers, design journalists, or entrepreneurs in the design field, their passion for the subject has brought me to want to know more about their work; their lives; their experience of design, and how they have managed to succeed in the complex sociopolitical situation in Poland.

I remember discussing the idea with my friend, photographer Dario Lombardi, and talking about the possibility of capturing this passion and energy, and bringing it together in a book.

Together with Anna Pietrzyk-Simone, we proposed this book project to the Adam Mickiewicz Institute (IAM), and it was then that the idea evolved into a research project. IAM's enthusiasm and support, and that of all the other partners we have encountered on the way, has allowed an idea to materialise into the very book you are holding now.

Working on this book project, it has become apparent that it is not so much about the training people receive in design as in other disciplines, but it is about the passion they put into what they do.

This thread of energy has been a common theme in interviewing the women designers and is especially evident in the portraits taken by Dario. His photographs communicate and share with the reader the spontaneity and the energy of the conversations, and the individual personalities of the women.

Discovering Women in Polish Design is a collection of interviews and conversations. It's my intention that each interview reveals an aspect of design in Poland, as seen through the eyes of women working in the industry. The choice of creating two formats (question-and-answer and profile pieces) is to allow the voices and opinions of the designers to communicate honestly to the reader. Key considerations, points of view, and critique can then come directly from the protagonists themselves.

Primarily, the ambition of this book was to bring a flavour of the exciting Polish design scene to the UK and international audience. It has been included in POLSKA! YEAR, a year-long programme of events organised by the Adam Mickiewicz Institute to promote Polish culture in the UK, from May 2009 to May 2010. Its aim has since evolved to incorporate a glimpse of a fast-growing Polish design scene. To bring this unfolding story to the attention of international design communities and hopefully steer a debate about design and gender. As much as anything, creativity in Poland is a product of social circumstance: the lack of resources has led people to become more creative.

In the history of modern design, Poland had an influential role with groundbreaking graphic design and illustration, however not many people are aware of the incredible research and energy that went into the development of furniture and industrial design even during the stranglehold of the Communist regime. Presented after the following interviews and conversations are two essays, the first by Anna Frąckiewicz on Wanda Telakowska, the second by Anna Maga on Hanna Chwierut-Jasicka. They offer a significant insight into the passionate and laborious work of two key women in the history of Polish design.

Post-Communist era, Polish designers started to travel and experience education and design abroad. Many designers who graduated in Europe or the US are now returning and are getting involved in teaching and education, bringing back with them the skills they have learnt abroad. This has triggered an exciting transformation, the result of which no one can precisely anticipate. Certainly it has set in motion the mechanism of the design industry in a country with an advanced manufacturing infrastructure, which has always produced for other countries, and is now in the process of learning how to engage with home-grown talent.

Some people asked me how could an Italian be interested in Polish design? My answer is very simple and obvious, and in fact very Italian, I have followed my instinct and let the passion build. The small signs of change that inspired me to research further are not only beneficial to Polish designers, but will have a profound effect on the design community at large. The evolution of Polish design will bring a significant sea change, that focuses more on the designers as human beings rather than merely products of the design industry.

Discovering Women in Polish Design — **PREFACE BY GIAN LUCA AMADEI**

INTRODUCTION
Czesława Frejlich
Polish female designers – yesterday and today

) **The major role played by Polish women** in the social sphere is less a result of the equal rights movement than the country's challenging political situation that began in 1772. The loss of independence, the various uprisings and the First and Second World Wars meant that many women not only had to bring up children on their own, but also ensure their families' material welfare.

Under the Prussian and Russian partitions, where everything Polish was forbidden, they taught the successive generations their mother tongue and passed down knowledge about Polish culture and history. After the Second World War the new socialist system declared general equality, which included women. This was more visible in the declarations than in reality. Not many women held managerial positions, but the accessibility of schooling allowed girls to have an education. The dentist, teacher, and salesperson professions had a strong female presence, which was associated with low wages, and which made these jobs unattractive to men. 1989 has brought few real changes: women's earnings continue to be lower; managerial positions are still mainly occupied by men, and political parties pay little attention to equal gender representation. Consciousness is growing, however, in women themselves: the Women's Party has come into being; more women than men attend university, and many have established their own firms.

Few women worked as designers in the past, but some left a sizeable legacy. The Polish history of design features a comparatively large number of women involved in textiles design. In the inter-war period, Antoni Buszek organised groups of young, artistically untrained girls in the framework of the Cracow Workshops. Under his direction they designed and produced decorative batik fabrics. These were displayed in 1925 at the International Exhibition of Decorative and Industrial Arts in Paris, where they were honoured with the Grand Prix. The best-known batiks were produced by a pair of sisters: Józefa and Zofia Kogut. At the Warsaw 'Order' [Ład] Artists' Cooperative, various talented kilim designers had their place, including Karolina Mikołajczyk-Bułhakowa, Zofia Grodecka, Halina Karpińska, and Eleonora Plutyńska. With their trademark geometrical forms that inspired the art deco style, kilims were very popular in the 1920s and 1930s. There were a few production houses, in Cracow, Warsaw and Lwów – now Lviv, Ukraine – which met this demand, employing mainly women, some of whom worked as designers.

In this period, the most outstanding figure was Julia Keilowa, a sculptress by education. She designed both one-of-a-kind silver dishes with sophisticated, geometrical forms, and plated serial products turned out by several Warsaw firms. Her works are much sought-after and admired on the antiques market. We cannot describe this period without mentioning Barbara Brukalska, among the first generation of architects affiliated with the International Style avant-garde. She and her husband, Stanisław Sokołowski, also designed interiors, exhibitions and furniture. She was the first female professor of architecture at the Warsaw Technical Academy.

In post-war Poland, a new generation of designers came to the fore, with a greater showing of women. In the Fifties and Sixties printed fabrics was popular. Their abstract patterns and vivid colours were synonymous with modernity, both in opposition to the pre-war 'Order', and to the 'grey' products put forward by the Polish People's Republic's socialised industry. Cheap production costs favoured the establishment of small cooperative handicraft factories. The most interesting centre was Sopot (in northern Poland), where Józefa Wnukowa educated a group of young female designers, later known as the Sopot School. The second was the Industrial Design Institute in Warsaw, where both visual artists of the older generation and young graduates of arts schools produced lengths of fabrics in limited series, dictated by the fashions at the time, and sold these at the Institute's shop.

Another specialist area that allowed many women to show off their talents was furniture. Growing numbers of female graduates from the Interior Architecture faculties of six of the major academies of fine arts entered the professional sphere, and the relatively stable economic situation of the Sixties and Seventies allowed them to hold a position on the job market. Some good examples here are Teresa Kruszewska and Maria Chomentowska, who designed wooden furniture, often exploring the beauty of bent plywood. They were well aware of their consumers' expectations: light, comfortable and inexpensive furniture.

Here we might note that there has been many examples of married couples working as professional duos in Polish design. After the war: Lucyna and Kazimierz Kowalski (ceramics); Bogusława and Czesław Kowalski (furniture); Eryka Trzewik-Drost and Jan Sylwester Drost (glass), and Małgorzata and Wojciech Małolepszy (product design). And, although this list could be significantly extended, in the new generation include Anna Siedlecka and Radek Achramowicz (lighting), and Agata Kulik-Pomorska and Rafał Pomorski (product design). The female counterparts of which are interviewed on the following pages.

The feminisation of design faculties is a visible phenomenon in Poland. At the end of the Eighties, women made up one third of the student body; today they are in the majority in many academies. This phenomenon is even more evident in the interior architecture faculties. After graduating, many women change their professions – bringing up children for a few years can limit their professional activity, and it is not easy to return to a field where there is so much competition.

Some female graduates are successfully running their own design or design-production firms. I will only mention by way of example those who have won the Red Dot competition: Renata Kalarus has been successful in designing upholstered furniture (the Comma Chair was awarded this year) and Magda Lubińska, whose firm, Moho designs and produces carpets (awarded last year for the _mohohej!DIA rug). Both of whom feature in this book.

The younger generation, aided by contemporary prototype and production technologies, Internet sales, opportunities, and exhibitions, are designing and manufacturing their own products much more. This often gets their foot in the door, helps them create a reliable portfolio and exist on the job market. Female designers also take advantage of this opportunity. At this year's Good Design [Dobry Wzór] exhibition – an annual survey of the best-designed Polish products – work by Daria Burlińska and Katarzyna Okińczyc was displayed.

As in other professions, Polish female designers are showing more and more initiative. This is helped by their historically established resourcefulness; betterment and the spread of education; their openness to the world, and their increasing awareness of their own worth.

Interviews & Conversations ⟩

Magdalena Komar

Textile Designer

❭ Magdalena Komar is particularly thrilled about the developments her textile work has been taking recently. 'They are so different from traditional embroidery that I'm still trying to come up with a proper name for them,' she says, laying out her designs on the kitchen table. The series of incredibly fine embroideries are constructed from cut-out fabric. Clustered in the middle of A4 sheets of paper, they resemble the plan of a dense cityscape.

When they are delicately raised from the table, the laser-cut fabric strips and circles are transformed into a three-dimensional sculpture. Komar's assemblage of the random pieces has extruded the seemingly flat, white-framed embroidery to form a miniature landscape.

The fragile nature and intricate weaving of the embroideries capture the essence of Komar herself: the delicate balance she strikes between work and her private life. Komar has just finished a job working as art director on an advertisment for a Polish advertising company; creating costumes for a cinema production, and taking care of her two-year-old daughter Maya. When we met in Warsaw in February 2009, it was in a rare, quiet moment between jobs while Maya was out for a walk with her nanny in the nearby park.

Although Komar enjoys the process of creating characters for cinema production and the short, intense commitment required to work in the advertising industry, what fulfills her most is working on her textiles: 'it is my happiest time,' she says.

Parisian fashion houses buy Komar's embroidery designs in sets. They are used to inspire new trends and collections. Each one has the raw energy of a concept sketch and often goes on to be developed further for a haute couture dress, or a precious accessory. Her latest design has been bought by the studio that produces embroidery for Chanel, and will likely contribute towards next season's collection.

Though she sometimes commits pen to paper and sketches out some of her ideas, Komar is strongly drawn to working directly with the materials, and often the process follows on from there. 'I like to touch things, I am a very emotional person, and the work I do is very much to do with expressing my emotions,' she says. To this end, Komar uses fabrics that are tactile and feminine, preferring to use silk and taffeta. 'When I graduated I worked with cotton, but it doesn't behave like silk: it doesn't have the same charm and sophistication,' explains Komar. Once she has bought the fabrics, Komar sends them to a laser-cutting company in southern Poland. 'People at the factory think I'm a bit odd,' she says. 'I am the lady that gets thousands of circles cut.' It is hard to picture Komar, who is a whirlwind of energy, calmly sitting down and meticulously stitching together minuscule pieces of fabric. But she is both a powerhouse of experimental ideas and also a deeply dedicated worker.

Komar's research into geometric shapes has been thorough yet instinctive. Her most recent experiments focus on circles and strips. Komar's animated personality is reflected in the intensive research she carries out, and, since she touches on a variety of ideas, her output is broad and very fast. 'I would like to be able to develop each design further, but I have to keep producing sets in order to sell ideas,' explains Komar. 'I don't have a studio yet, which is an advantage in a way, so that I can be with Maya while working.'

Komar left Poland in her early 20's to study fashion at the Ecole Supérieure des Arts et techniques de la Mode (Esmod) in Paris, and specialised in textile design. 'At that stage my textiles were closer to fine art,' she recalls. 'They were like little sculptures and weren't accepted by my tutors because the school was more fashion-based.'

After graduating, Komar moved back to Warsaw where she started working as a costume designer for cinema and as a stylist for music videos. 'After three years, though, I felt it was time to do something with my textiles,' she says. Komar left for England in 2001 and began a BA in Multimedia Textiles at Loughborough University. 'The course was fantastic as I was pushed to experiment and research all the time,' says Komar. 'I remember being stuck on the campus and finally I had the time to focus on what I loved most: textiles.'

For her final project she designed prints inspired by Aubrey Beardsley, the British illustrator famous for his work on Oscar Wilde's Salomé. The project was selected for the New Designers show at the Business Design Centre in London in 2003. Having refined her own style at Loughborough, Komar went back to Paris where she started to sell to Chanel. She also took an internship at Christian Lacroix, helping with the haute couture collection, and worked with long-time employer Atelier Montex, the embroidery studio that bought her first designs.

In 2004, Komar also started making handmade satin silk scarves, which quickly formed a collection. 'These pieces are not trendy at all,' she says. 'I stitched them one by one.' This collection also expresses Komar's love for geometric shapes. Her high-octane output came to a standstill for more than two and a half years, however, when she became pregnant with Maya. 'I wasn't able to keep the rhythm of the work I was juggling,' she explains. Although Maya's arrival put most work on hold for a while, Komar continued with the cinema projects in Poland. 'For one of the productions I had to create characters based on old people, so I would take Maya for a stroll in Warsaw's Moczydło Park, and study faces there for my characters, taking notes and photos,' she says. Indeed, Komar's motherhood has enhanced her drive to

be creative. How she finds time is another matter. Maya's father is English and works in documentary distributions, so the three of them spend time in both London and Warsaw. 'I love Poland, and I think I am really Polish,' she says. 'In fact, I feel even more Polish when I'm in England.'

As the buzzer announces the return of little Maya and her nanny, we move to a bedroom where the floor is transformed into a work surface. Komar lays out more 3D embroideries, more rigorous than the previous ones and with a strong reference to Japanese design. Inspecting each one is like holding rare parchment, though Komar is not precious about her work. Each piece is constructed with an incredible intricacy and intensity, which signifies the other side of Komar's personality: a woman with profound passion and dedication in her work and life. 'When I sell my work to fashion houses I have to make sure my designs strike a balance between the traditional and the experimental,' she explains, as if describing her own tendencies. 'Often, if the design is very logical, people will buy it.'

Although Komar juggles her personal life and jobs between cities, she is keen to set up a studio and dedicate more time to fewer ideas. 'I would love to take my 3D experimental embroideries beyond fashion,' she says. 'It would be wonderful to move them into architecture or interiors, and experience their impact on a larger scale.'

Maja Ganszyniec
Product designer

) I knew that Maja Ganszyniec had moved back to Poland in October 2008 after completing her Masters in product design at the Royal College of Art (RCA) in London, but I didn't know why. I was intrigued to find out about her experience at the RCA and how it had affected her view on design. We met at the Przegryź restaurant in the centre of Warsaw. It was a late-winter's morning and the city was still covered in snow.

GA When did you decide to train as a designer?

MG For me, everything started with maths and physics at high school: I realised that wasn't something I wanted to do in my life. Instead I wanted to work in the creative arts and took a place at the Academy of Fine Arts in Cracow studying interior architecture. The school was specialist, but also limited in its processes of investigation and analysis.

During my fourth year I had a great opportunity to go to the Milan Politecnico as part of the European student exchange programme, Erasmus. The school itself was a huge, very complex and bureaucratic institution, and in terms of work it did not much to offer, so very soon I started to look for something outside. After one-week workshop with Alessandro Mendini, I applied for work experience in his office and ended up spending three months there. It was perfect timing for me as the studio was working on the first exhibition of Mendini's work in Poland, to be held at the National Museum in Poznań in 2004.

After the internship, my Erasmus programme was over, but just before going back I did another workshop with the architect Luca Scacchetti. I remember that everyone was working on computers. So when I made this cardboard scale model and did sketches by hand, Scacchetti saw it he said, "oh my God, you are a terrorist!" I was confused, I couldn't work out whether he liked it or hated it. "You don't work this way at the Politecnico," he said. "I want you in my office." So I stayed for another four months working in his studio, before I returned to Cracow to finish my degree and start work as a freelance interior designer.

GA Why did you go to the RCA?

MG It was a few months after my graduation, in the middle of the Polish winter, I was standing on a building site in –20°C, shouting at construction workers who had just built a wall in the wrong place, and I realised that this was not the right thing for me. So I thought: what is the best (although also the most improbable) thing that could happen to me – getting a place at the RCA. I applied to do an MA in product design and just left it there. I was broke at the time when I got accepted. It was a trying period, and I was close to giving up on numerous occasions, but every time something came my way to help me out. Somehow it always works out if you really know what you want.

GA What did you enjoy most during your time at the RCA?

MG You're like a little plant in the greenhouse of the college: they water you and you grow in a perfect work environment. The two years at the RCA were incredibly hard, but also incredibly fruitful. The most important thing there is the people: I spent all my time with amazing, driven, young designers from various backgrounds. We talked about projects not only in the studio, but over a coffee in the cafe, or a beer in the bar and every idea is re-evaluated. These two years changed my way of working and thinking. There is no college in Poland that would provide such facilities: a well-equipped workshop; an amazing library, and an open field for experimental work.

GA Was that a revelation for you?

MG Yes. My previous design education experience in Italy and Poland was all computer-based: the project is ready when the rendering is ready, which is all wrong. Each object you design occupies a real space and has its own presence, you have to build it physically to be able to understand it. The problem with 3D modelling is that it stops the project when it should begin. The real design process, the investigation,

MG I have never lived in Warsaw before. It took me about six months to familiarise myself with the know-how of the place, and I speak the language! At the moment I am working on furniture, exhibition and product design, and I'm looking to open a studio in collaboration with other designers soon.

Things are happening here, design is a new and exciting subject, now is a good time for young, creative people. There are so many things to do; anything you look at in the street is a design subject. Changes are already happening in the Polish education system. Young and talented people, such as Tomek Rygalik are now teaching at the Academy of Fine Arts in Warsaw. I hope other colleges will understand that this is the right direction, and the only way to reach a European level of education.

Sometimes it is upsetting and frustrating to work here where many producers, especially small ones, still don't think they need a designer. They don't want to take the risk: it's better to produce another kitchen than an interesting piece of furniture. I hope it's only a matter of time before they understand that design and innovation shifts into money. Being a designer here and now offers a unique opportunity to take part in the creation of the design market. I believe that in four or five years things will be great here. There's still a lot to do and it's time to turn the problems into possibilities.

research and analysis, is often missing or limited to mere styling.

GA Why did you come back to Warsaw?

MG I didn't really plan to be back in Warsaw so soon. Just after my graduation I came here with one bag, more for a holiday than anything else. Then a few things happened and I realised that I needed a break after these two years of working 24/7. Being inside this madness it's hard to get the right perspective on what you do. I wanted to understand which direction to follow.

It was the most unexpected decision to come back, but I am glad I did as Poland is a very exciting place for design at the moment. I remember at the RCA, I had a conversation about my work with Deyan Sudjic, director of London's Design Museum. He asked me why my designs were so safe and legible. "It was my choice," I said. I was building a portfolio that would be understood in Poland, as I was planning to go back there at some point. In the UK everything has already been designed whereas in Poland we are now aiming at things that happened in some parts of Europe in the Seventies in terms of design.

GA How do you relate to the design community in Warsaw now? Are things changing in the industry and in education?

—— Being a designer here and now offers a unique opportunity to take part in the creation of the design market ——

Ewa Gołębiowska

Director of the Silesian Castle of Art and Enterprise

〉 I met Ewa Gołębiowska in October 2007 in Cieszyn, Silesia, on my first trip to Poland. I was instantly enchanted by her energy. My interview with her took place in January 2008, on the third anniversary of the Silesian Castle of Art and Enterprise: it was the end of a long and emotional day for Gołębiowska, having organised the event for a number of guests including designers, lecturers, and local government representatives.

We sat and talked in the tea house, her favourite part of the Castle. When we arrived, a small group of friends were there waiting for her and it felt as though I knew them too. We drank white tea in small Japanese porcelain cups, and it felt like we were removed from any particular space or time.

GA How did you get involved in the design world?
EG I have always been interested in design and art, especially modern art, however I am not a trained designer. I belong to the generation born in the late Fifties, that was in its 20's during Solidarity in Poland. It was a good generation, one that believed things could change here. I still have this belief. At the time, a lot of my friends were active in politics and culture and I am still very proud of that moment in Polish history.

I studied the Polish language in Cracow and than came back to Cieszyn, where I have lived and worked ever since. I taught in primary school in a small village nearby, which I was happy doing because I felt I was helping young people and children to grow up. There was an exceptional Mayor at the time, who believed that what makes a great town isn't its size, but how interesting it is: what happens in the town, and how open people are. In my opinion, Cieszyn is quite an open place. Firstly because there's a mix of religions, not just Protestant and Catholic, but about 15 other beliefs. Secondly, it is a border town, which immediately makes it more open.

Coming back to Polish design and my way into it: there are, of course, people who are able to plan their life and who are able to realise their plan, but in my opinion life is much more interesting if you keep your curiosity alive and stay open to possibilities.

After working in primary education, I got a job in Cieszyn
  Town Hall heading up the Education, Sport and Tourism
  Department. Every day I'd tell myself that my task was to
  find a way of realising good ideas. Good design has a similar
  aim. Here in Poland we need good design. This means that
  we need better products to develop our manufacturing
  industry and survive this cruel global market. It would also
  produce more jobs and a better quality of life. But design
  also means a chance to improve people's lives. Not in
  terms of luxury goods (of course we love them because for
  so many years we couldn't buy anything in the shops), but
  design also means better public spaces, which have been
  neglected in Poland especially.

We need a huge movement here to improve the quality of our
  environment; the safety of our roads; the safety of our
  homes, and all this is also connected to design. We really
  are just at the beginning of a long journey.

GA Is the Silesian Castle of Art and Enterprise the starting point
  for this movement you mention?
EG Everything needs to be designed here in Poland, starting
  with objects that are part of our daily life, such as
  uncomfortable street furniture, complicated instructions
  and train tickets with too much information printed on
  them. They were all made without design thinking.

This just shows how much we could improve our lives through creativity and good design.

The Castle has begun to organise a popular project Design in Public Space, as well as gatherings, focused on important issues such as communication, safety and accessibility. This initiative is looking for the cross-over point between art and business, and this is design. I feel that this is also part of my mission with the Castle. From the offset, this local initiative wasn't only to promote design, but to help companies to cooperate with designers. We conducted research among manufacturers and designers and the result was what we expected: businesses in Poland do not understand what design is. Businesses are confident about the necessity of product development and market sales, but not design.

What we are trying to do with the Castle initiative is to have lots of exhibitions, not showing design as a luxury, or a commodity, but design for the everyday. The kind of industrial design that is not well known in Poland, such as engineering, production, and even packaging, which has only recently been recognised as design. To show and promote the best crop of designers in the region we organise the annual regional design competition Silesian Icons. This helps a lot of local designers gain exposure and let local people get closer to design.

GA How did you initiate the Castle Enterprise?

EG I haven't trained as a designer, so I sought knowledge from design experts and academics. Working on the proposal for the Castle I've also learnt that with design, as with business, you can only propose something of the best quality, so I knew I needed the best people for Cieszyn. We have a team and network of national and international experts, who we meet with every three months to discuss problems, obstacles, successes, and even failures.

We received money from the EU to start up the initiative. Everything has to be very carefully planned and promoted because we need to show the results at the end of every year. This initiative really began by chance. Three of us were working together and wanted to do something to bring about change in Cieszyn and Polish design. The best idea for the initiative happened to be discussed at Sunday lunch over a chocolate cake: a very informal meeting. Then the following day we tested out the idea on the Mayor of Cieszyn and the Silesian Marshal's Office (Urząd Marszałkowski), and from then on we started to work with architects and on the feasibility studies to physically refurbish the castle to become the Silesian Castle of Art and Enterprise.

GA How difficult has it been for you as a woman to fight for initiating something that's so different and forward-looking in terms of design and business?

EG I have quite a lot of courage and self confidence. It's not a problem of gender, the problem is how much you really believe in the idea you want to make a reality. Since the beginning I've been positive that it's a good idea, and also good for the town, for the region and for design and its associated businesses. The development of the Castle is possibly the most important thing that has happened in my life, maybe because I didn't plan it. It's the adventure of my life and I'm in a comfortable position because my family appreciates this and supports me, so I can do it. The other people I work with at the Castle are dreamers and hard workers like me. It's very important to have this combination of ideals and discipline. There isn't really any other way for things to get done.

GA Did you realise what you were tapping into when you set up the initiative for the Castle?

EG I just knew how much Polish design needed an initiative like this. There is a heritage and value there, which has been almost completely lost. I can tell you that in the World Exhibition held in Paris in 1925 and 1937, Polish artists and applied arts and architecture got as many medals as the Scandinavians, but in every shop and supermarket in Finland you'll find Alvar Aalto glass, and Maija Isola fabric. They kept it as a national heritage, they use it and wear it; they have it at home, and they sit on these design pieces. Whereas in Poland, the course of history played against design. There was war and Stalinism in the Fifties, and we lost everything. Now we have very talented young designers, but 80% of them can find jobs overseas, whereas in the Eighties and Nineties I didn't have the opportunity to work abroad. It is their personal choice to stay here and help build their own country, or go where life is more comfortable but maybe also less interesting.

Marta Białecka
+ Anna Piwowar
Product and graphic designers

) Marta Białecka and Anna Piwowar are two quite opposite but equally fantastic characters. They tell me that at school they hated each other. Professionally, however, they really complement one another. Białecka is lively and talkative, while Piwowar is more subdued. Their diverse personalities come across in their beautifully crafted work, which is playful yet considered. During our conversation in a cafe in Warsaw, many pertinent issues emerge in relation to design in Poland, the education system and the relationship between designers and manufacturers. Truly insightful, the conversation helped me to better understand the dramatic changes underway in Polish design.

GA Why did you call yourself La Polka?

MB We wanted to define ourselves, our identity, and be as open as possible, so we decided to refer to things that are certain: we are women and we are from Poland. "La" is the feminine article in French, and "Polka" means Polish woman. It's easy to remember.

GA When did you start up your business?

MB Actually we started working together when we were still studying industrial design at the Academy of Fine Arts in Warsaw. We did some projects together back then and somehow, quite naturally, it became a more serious cooperation, with clients and real jobs. Anna feels she's better at graphics, while I'm a bit better at making 3D forms, so it's a good balance.

GA Do you find it a problem making a living from your work?

MB Yes. We could be called "ghost" designers because we're not for real: we don't have the opportunity to work as full-time product designers in Poland. So we have day jobs as graphic designers to earn money. But when it comes to our products we have to be really motivated, you need a lot of determination to work as a designer in Poland. It's not easy here, first you have to build up experience.

GA Do you mean the Polish market is not ready to work with designers?

MB Exactly. We have a funny situation here in which there are more and more talented and original designers, and we also have people who want to own nice things by these Polish designers. We also have magazines that are eager to write about these designers. But what we don't have is the kind of market that would let designers do their work, and design. It's funny because we have the two sides set up, but not the bit in the middle.

GA What do you think is the key element that will change the current situation?

MB I think it will take some work at government level. We should have some encouragement on a national level. We have these things that happen, for example, the competitions organised by Elle Decoration, that are meant to marry designers with manufacturers, but it doesn't seem to work very effectively.

GA Why?

MB Maybe just because it takes time. It's one thing creating an artificial situation whereby you meet manufacturers, but our background and the reality that we live in doesn't really foster this cooperation. We can meet and discuss how lovely it would be, but when the manufacturer gets home and looks at the figures, he thinks better of it.

GA In these situations there has to be some alchemy, you can't necessarily control them. It's like speed dating between the designer and the manufacturer. It only works up to a point.

MB Absolutely. It should be a natural need in the market. There should come a time when there is a real need for designers working in a company and then it will take off. But until this magical point I don't know if we can force it to happen. Probably not. It's just a process that has to evolve.

GA What made you stay in Poland rather than anywhere else in Europe?

MB There are definitely some advantages to being in Poland now. Firstly, as designers it's still quite cheap and convenient to make prototypes, for example. Not if it's something that should be made from a high-tech material, but when it comes to simple stuff you can find people who will do it for you. Of course they won't necessarily do it quite right, but they will do it. So this is a good thing.

Marta Białecka

Anna Piwowar

Some German designers have their prototypes made in Poland, and they think we are very lucky. It's very nice because if we were out in Italy or England probably we wouldn't have been noticed. But in Poland everything is new and people want this information about new designers, about design in general, and they want to read about it.

GA You both studied and set up your practice in Warsaw, did you travel around Europe to get a sense of what is happening across the border in terms of design?

MB I'm constantly thinking about it. We love travelling not only to see design, but also to see art, which to me is the ultimate source of inspiration, and to observe the people and experience everyday situations in a completely different environment. We usually go to Paris or New York, these seem to be our most influential cities. I find Marcel Duchamp a great inspiration and I have always been fascinated by abstract painting, especially geometric abstraction. I must say after my last visit to New York I started to really appreciate abstract expressionism. I've always been a fan of Isamu Noguchi, whose works are among the most successful examples of the meeting of East and West. My big dream, though, is to go to Japan, since Japanese design demonstrates a sensitivity to form, and a certain devotion and discipline to it that manifests in a total withdrawal of a designer's ego from the work. That's what I consider a total mastery: a design that seems like it has just emerged naturally, without human interference.

GA Regarding your design process, how do you initiate a project, do you work without a client and set up your own brief?

MB Well, it comes back to ghost designing because we don't have these real situations. We don't have the clients, the market and the real needs that we should respond to. We generally design for ourselves or for competitions and exhibitions. It's not a real situation. It's all about thinking and ideas. For example, some of the designs that we've made for My World: The New Subjectivity in Design at The National Art Gallery Zachęta were created specially for the exhibition, so they weren't functional.

The truth is that the most realistic designs that I've made were during my studies. We had these artificial situations but they were very strict. We had a profile of the end-user and the whole process, and we had to answer certain criteria. It's funny that the education system makes you deal with a reality that somehow doesn't exist. You can't really learn a profession when your teachers only have experience from a local and very specific market.

GA So something needs to change in the Polish education system?

MB I don't think that's the main problem, I think it's the market. That's the point where it should all start. When you have a market that is developed enough to need design, then you have this natural situation in which designers do work, and they can teach real design, and students have real jobs after graduation. And they can cooperate with some companies during their studies, which of course we did, with Ikea and Hans Grohe, but it wasn't enough. It changes so fast, though. Students now have more opportunities and more real situations to deal with than we did.

GA But there's no school that can teach you about the real world.

MB Yes, that's true, but then again doing things like working in practice, and teaching people about the legal side, about prices for example, all these things you should know when you complete an MA. Design is about constantly thinking about what you do. To me, it's very important to be self-critical because you always have to think about the people on the other side and predict their reaction.

GA But when it comes to working in the real world, it's really rewarding. It's about growing and moving forward and gaining new experiences.

MB Which is what I was talking about when I explained the reason for our name. We didn't want to make up a name that would define us in a specific sector of design, instead we wanted a name that would make us instantly recognisable and give us the freedom to work across all areas of design. It is very much about keeping all options open and challenging our design skills.

Discovering Women in Polish Design — **MARTA BIAŁECKA + ANNA PIWOWAR**

Anna Łoskiewicz
+ Zofia Strumiłło-Sukiennik

Product designers

Anna Łoskiewicz

Zofia Strumiłło-Sukiennik

) Out of all the Polish designers I met, Łoskiewicz and
Strumiłło-Sukiennik are the most immersed in the city
where they live and work. For the women behind design
practice Beza Projekt, Warsaw's complex history, pace
and urban fabric is inspirational. In conversation,
Łoskiewicz and Strumiłło-Sukiennik's words convey
the energy of the Polish capital. It was appropriate,
therefore, that our meeting took place in what could be
described as the heart of Warsaw, the 1955 Palace of
Culture and Science, a gift from the Soviet Union.

In 2003, Łoskiewicz and Strumiłło-Sukiennik graduated from
the Faculty of Industrial Design at the Academy of Fine
Arts in Warsaw. That same year they founded their
design studio, although the duo prefer to be considered
'creative people' rather than 'designers', which they
believe is a restrictive definition.

Though they echo each other's ambition and passion, it is
clear even at first glance that they are very different
characters. Strumiłło-Sukiennik appears settled and
calm, while Łoskiewicz is more introverted yet direct
in expressing her views. Both women are involved in
outside projects. Strumiłło-Sukiennik teaches in the same
department where she was educated in Warsaw, as well
as working with her husband Jan Sukiennik at 137kilo,
an architecture and design collective. Łoskiewicz is the
creative director for major graphic design studio, Brain,
in Warsaw, and is involved in a series of other projects
and disciplines, including photography, which she
studied in Poznań after her first degree.

Like many Polish designers, Łoskiewicz and Strumiłło-
Sukiennik share the troubled destiny of a split life
between a day job and running a design practice. The
upside to this situation is that they are able to initiate
their own projects, which facilitates a certain amount
of freedom. However, this is costly and they often find
themselves frustrated by not having time to get some
of their ideas into production, and see a return of their
initial investments.

Łoskiewicz and Strumiłło-Sukiennik's way of working is loaded with an instinctive and inspiring raw energy, which could be mistaken for naivety. 'Sometimes we move very fast from one project to another,' says Łoskiewicz. 'One moment we'll be intensely involved in a project, the next we'll have already moved on to developing another idea. Sometimes we leave things unfinished, or not as thoroughly explored as we would like. We're well aware of this, though, and are trying to rectify it by being more commercially minded.'

Besides putting together a business plan for their studio, Łoskiewicz and Strumiłło-Sukiennik develop challenging designs, which subvert everyday objects, such as a table or a stool. Beza Projekt's intention is to trigger people's own creativity by encouraging people to take an alternative approach to how they view their surrounding environment.

'We like playing with changing the function of things,' says Strumiłło-Sukiennik. 'Most of the projects we do as Beza originate from our creativity, intuitions and interests. We work as though we are the client, and when we attend art events and design fairs we design and construct the prototypes ourselves.'

Beza's projects respond directly to the city. 'There are many places in the suburbs of Warsaw, for example, where we like to potter around,' says Łoskiewicz. 'You can come across some unbelievable shops, where you can really measure people's creativity. There are some wonderful discoveries to be made, like a gigantic strawberry as part of a shop display. Things that if they were in an art gallery could be a piece by Jeff Koons.'

As much as they like this hidden identity of Warsaw, they are also aware that they are witnesses to a fading history. Increasingly, old buildings in the city are making space for new retail and luxury residential units. Many Polish citizens still have a negative attachment towards things produced under the Communist regime. 'People have the perception that the loss of identity in Poland happened during this time,' says Łoskiewicz. 'But I don't think it's as much to do with Communism as with switching over to a free market. People suddenly felt free, they felt that everything was possible. It was a crazy time, lots of nice buildings were destroyed in Warsaw, and the city started to get covered with advertisements. You can't see the architecture, only billboards.'

Strumiłło-Sukiennik explains to me that the majority of Poles have an aversion to minimal design, or anything remotely

Discovering Women in Polish Design — **ANNA ŁOSKIEWICZ + ZOFIA STRUMIŁŁO-SUKIENNIK** connected with modernism. Inevitably, this attitude underpins the criticism aimed at the understated design of the forthcoming Warsaw Museum of Modern Art by Swiss architect Christian Kerez. 'Many people would have preferred a wild and colourful scheme, instead of something minimal that reminds them of the difficult time in the Sixties,' says Strumiłło-Sukiennik. 'Poles are still so sensitive about that unfortunate period that they reject everything associated with it, including excellent examples of architecture in Warsaw. This will slowly change.'

Despite the perception of the recent Polish architecture heritage, Łoskiewicz and Strumiłło-Sukiennik feel that Warsaw is the place to be for designers. 'I recently spent six months in Berlin,' says Łoskiewicz. 'It might have something to do with staying in the west part of the city, but I was bored. Maybe because everything is too regimented there. Nothing was as organic as it is in Warsaw.'

My impression of Łoskiewicz and Strumiłło-Sukiennik is of a pair clearly in love with their city, and encouraged by the opportunities it has to offer creative people like themselves. 'All the inspiration we need is right here, and we really appreciate that,' says Łoskiewicz, as Strumiłło-Sukiennik nods in affirmation. 'We really feel that we're learning from the ugliness of the city, and we can see its beauty and the possibilities it holds.'

Agnieszka Jacobson-Cielecka
Journalist and curator

) I met Agnieszka Jacobson-Cielecka for the first time in Warsaw in October 2007 during a study trip organised by the Adam Mickiewicz Institute. Jacobson-Cielecka was one of the people who inspired me to put this book project together. As founding editor of Elle Decoration Poland, Jacobson-Cielecka pioneered intensive research into emerging Polish designers and helped to promote them in the magazine. During our conversation, we focused on the current situation of the media in Poland. After leaving Elle Decoration in 2007, Jacobson-Cielecka pursued a freelance career, which has given her the opportunity to fulfill her mission to help promote and develop Polish design. Jacobson-Cielecka is also curating the Łódź Design Festival for the second time this year and recently initiated the Natural Resources of Polish Design exhibition at the Regional Museum of Stalowa Wola, as well as Unpolished, Young Design From Poland (Brussels, 2009).

GA How did you start working for Elle Decoration Poland?

AJC I started at Elle in 1994. After my first child was born I had to look for a part-time job and ended up taking a position as a stylist for the magazine, which I did for a long time before I started writing. The magazine had just launched in Poland and they were working on the third issue when I joined. I had studied fine art and I was really intrigued by the idea of working with still-life objects in a different way to what I had been doing as a painter.

At the time, there was nothing about design in Poland and it was great to have the opportunity to travel to international fairs like Milan. I had been at the magazine for three years when I decided to look closely at the Polish design scene and found that design existed in Poland after all! In 2001, together with Beata Bochińska, president of the board at the Industrial Design Institute, we launched Prodeco, a competition for producers, distributors and young designers. I am proud to see that our winners – students at the time – have emerged as a strong new generation of internationally recognised designers.

My first ambition was to introduce a design consciousness in Poland, the second was to discover design in Poland, and I had managed to do both. Unfortunately this has changed now, as there is a stronger emphasis on pushing readers to shop rather than inform them about design.

GA The media clearly has the power to push sales. It must have been very interesting to assist in the shift that has happened in Poland since 1989 and be a part of people learning how to make informed decisions about buying products?

AJC Magazines tend to show what people want to see. In my opinion, though, magazines should aim to publish more challenging and avant-garde items and stories in order to push their readership to look harder and deeper. One problem with this approach could be that if something is too difficult to understand, it might push the readers towards something much easier, and less stimulating.

GA This situation doesn't really help designers in Poland to push the boundaries of design.

AJC It all depends on the way publications present innovative design products and projects. The point is to introduce the readers to design concepts, which will challenge them in a friendly way.

GA Do you think it makes things more complicated that there are so few Polish manufacturers working with Polish designers?

AJC Most designers in Poland have to work two jobs to pay their bills, in graphic design or advertising, for example. Some designers have decided to become their own producers. The industry here in Poland is not prepared and educated in design: it's not able to trust designers yet. We need more design management skills here to help resolve this issue. For some reason many Polish manufacturers are afraid of taking risks. They are more interested in doing something similar to what's already in production, rather than a completely new product.

Polish furniture manufacturer Iker is a very interesting example. This company is not investing much in advertising, but instead it's focusing on design: pushing production and Polish designers. Its approach has attracted the attention of Polish design publications, resulting in large editorial coverage. People working in design all thought this was a smart move on Iker's part. This is the right way of stimulating creativity and getting Polish design into production.

managed to get one, you didn't really care about the shape or the colour because you were glad just to have one.

Surprisingly, though, during the Communist period we did have design and designers were working hard using the state facilities. Nothing reached production but now we have a vast design collection of prototypes that belongs to the National Museum. Most of the material is currently in storage, the museum is in the process of finding new exhibition spaces to bring the collection to the public. Then the task will be to build more educational programmes for design in Poland, like the ones in place at the British Museum or London's Victoria and Albert Museum, which are free and accessible to everyone.

GA Having left your post at Elle Decoration to pursue a freelance career, what plans do you have for the future?

AJC It feels very new, it seems I have more possibilities, even in publishing. I am writing a lot for Polish magazines, I believe that writing for a wide public could support design more than exclusive or specialist niche magazines. However, I am writing for those as well. My dream is to initiate Design Week in Warsaw. I think it is a shame that the city still has nothing like it. However, I am very happy about the positive response the Łódź Design Festival has received since my involvement in it as a curator. First of all, though, we will need to learn more about how to cooperate with each other to make sure the Polish design community continues to grow and gain local and international recognition.

Unfortunately, those producers who took the challenge of design haven't had commercial success because people are still buying old-fashioned pieces. And it is a mission for magazines to make people realise the necessity of design. Even if the industry decides to implement design into production, if they aren't able to sell it they will stop. This is the media's most important role: to help people become aware of design and make it clear that design is not only about having gadgets, but much more about a quality of life.

GA The same happened in Italy in the late Fifties: Italian manufacturers looked up to Scandinavian design and tried to produce something similar. It took someone like Gio Ponti to push Italian manufacturers to find their own identity.

AJC Some companies don't have any ambition to produce more because they are already producing for foreign trade. They don't care about their own name as such, because they are producing for bigger, more prestigious furniture companies.

I think it's just a matter of time, though. I started working in design in 1994 when we had only three or four specialised shops in Warsaw. We've grown so much in 15 years. People are now travelling a lot and our knowledge and attitude toward design is growing faster than the market. If you observe people and people's needs, you realise how fast it's all changing. We didn't really have anything before 1989. If you wanted a sofa and you

Magdalena Lubińska
Founder of Moho Design

) This book project is in part thanks to Magda Lubińska as she was my first point of contact with the Polish design scene. The first time I met Lubińska was during the London Design Festival in 2007 at Moroso's opening of their new London showroom. While inspecting the unusual design of one of the rugs on display, Lubińska came close to me and asked if I liked the piece. I said that I did and told her I was intrigued to know about the technique they had used to manufacture it. We started to talk and I was introduced to her partner Michał Biernacki who had designed the rug collection. Before I knew it, in October 2007 I was travelling to Cieszyn on my first trip to Poland.

GA How did Moho Design come about?

ML When I was nine months pregnant with Pola, I was preparing the nest, as mothers-to-be usually do, and decorating the house. When it came to buying a carpet for my flat, I couldn't find what I was looking for, so I decided I would design one myself. I researched into local businesses and manufacturers around where I am based, in the Silesian region in southern Poland, and I finally came across one factory producing woven felt, which is still used to make trousers by the Polish highlanders called Górale living between Silesia and northern Slovakia. It turns out it is a fantastic material, really inspiring and versatile. So, following my intuition I thought, I'm going to go for it – I was so excited about this new project that I gave birth two weeks early. When Pola was two weeks old, I was already

43

in the factory creating the colour palettes and putting together the team of people who would do the first collection. I remember breastfeeding Pola in the factory.

GA When I came across Moho Design I felt that along with using a very traditional material to develop something new in design, there was a very clear and clever marketing operation driving it, which has helped Moho to be recognised at an international level. Can you say a bit more about that?

ML I studied Law, not design. I left my studies when I realised that it wasn't the career I wanted to pursue. When I entered the world of design I wasn't actually trained as a designer, so it was all about following my intuition. Before founding Moho in 2004, I set up my own advertising agency but I felt quite restricted and couldn't use my passion for creativity and design. The Moho studio has really given me the freedom to be creative. So, to answer your question, I must say I don't see marketing as separate from the products, or design, but I see it as a complete picture where each component is equally relevant and essential.

GA Is there a design scene where Moho is based in Katowice, or do you need to go to Cracow or Warsaw to be part of the Polish design community?

ML I need to go to London and Milan for fresh ideas, not Warsaw or Cracow. Katowice, the city where I live and work is in the Silesia region, which was renowned for coal mining. Now that this industry is dying, the creative and design industry is growing in its place, and design studios, advertising agencies and architecture practices ared dotted around the whole region. I remember asking Ewa [Gołębiowska] why there are so many interesting, creative people coming from such a grey and, lets face it, ugly place? And apparently there is a very good architectural school near Katowice, in Gliwice. So now it seems the best Polish architects and designers are coming out of Silesia.

GA Speaking to other Polish designers it has emerged that in Poland there are many problems trying to put designs into production. You have been very brave in starting your own business. There are other designers in Poland who are very talented but seem worried to go all the way, and take risks. What's your view on this?

ML I think it is almost impossible to be a designer and producer at the same time, if you are a producer you have certain restrictions: you need a low price and a healthy margin to make money. For me, a design company needs a visionary product designer, who believes in design, as well as an equally visionary manager. We only need to think of Apple: the well-established collaboration between a visionary product designer, such as Jonathan Ive, and a visionary entrepreneur, such as Steven Jobs.

When I think about the example that Moho has set for Polish designers I feel a bit guilty. Its success may have led many young designers in Poland to think that they can do it on their own, starting off their own productions and designs independently, rather than engaging with existing manufacturers. The reason behind Moho's success was being in the right place at the right time. It was a good concept, but I also had lots of people who contributed to the company's success all the way through.

GA Do you think that designers in Poland could and should challenge local manufacturers?

ML Industrial design in Poland is taught in art schools, so they are mostly trained as artists. On the other side you have engineers, for example, who receive a more practical training. They end up speaking two different technical languages, which results in fragmented communication. Unfortunately, designers can't communicate with marketing people because of the same problem. So there's no knowledge of how to prepare the product for production, or how to manage the prototyping phase. Right now in Poland design is very much about conceptual aesthetic work, with little thought going into how to further develop a new design product. This disparateness ultimately ends in missing the market and the end-user.

GA Is it all down to communication?

ML Poland has a strong design heritage that only got as far as the prototype stage.

GA Where did you draw your inspiration from?

ML When I set up Moho Design and the carpet studio, I really wanted

—— A company needs a visionary product designer who believes in design, as well as an equally visionary manager ——

the business to have a strong identity. It wasn't my intention to create an international brand, but I know I wanted to create something that had Polish roots. I wasn't particularly aware of Polish design from the Fifties and Sixties, so I studied folk motifs. I chose to bring these to life by creating a contemporary interpretation, in order to maintain that tradition with my Polish heritage.

Lots of Polish designers are looking at tradition but focusing mainly on the period before 1900, and there's a gap in the intervening years, where no one knows what happened. Since Moho rediscovered folk motifs, other designers have taken the same route. I am aware that obviously it was used before, but not on such a successful scale. When Moho started to become internationally renowned, that was the time when here almost no one knew about design. The fact that Moho became a marketing and PR success has helped me connect with big, serious manufacturers who believe I am the right person from a business, as well as a design, point of view.

GA And what do you see as the direction of Moho now?

ML My job of creating Moho is done in a way, and there are other people contributing to the company. We definitely want to work with international designers and develop new products.

GA It's really interesting that Moho was a way of starting a process.

ML I didn't have any restrictions, I was completely free, perhaps if I had written a business plan and come to the whole thing with a pen and paper, in a more rational way, I wouldn't have done what I have done. I probably wouldn't have had the courage to do it.

GA But in your case you were looking for something that was missing and you created it. Intuition is the amazing part of the design process.

ML I think I was very lucky because I didn't study design and didn't have any restrictions imposed on me by that training. I also feel it is important to stay relevant both to the country you're living in, and also globally, and have a knowledge and an overview of what is going on around you. I think it's partly to do with our century, it's very fast-changing. It's hard to keep up, but you need to keep looking around and follow your intuition.

Renata Kalarus
Product designer

) Renata Kalarus' studio is a focal point of activity, brimming over with raw materials and work in progress. Kalarus is based in Cracow, in an ex-industrial building where she has a workshop, and a furniture and lighting showroom. 'The aim of the space is to become a hub of design in Cracow,' says Kalarus. 'Recently we had Premiery 2008 here. It's an exhibition featuring furniture by Polish designers such as Tomek Rygalik and Piotr Kuchciński, produced by Polish manufacturer Noti.'

It is a Saturday morning when we meet and Kalarus appears relaxed as I nose around her studio while she prepares a coffee on her dashing Nespresso machine. Scattered on a long table are some ceramic sculptures and other unfinished pieces by Kalarus' life and business partner, the sculptor and interior designer, Jerzy Cyganiewicz

Kalarus' straight dark hair is parted in the middle and partially covers her face as she explains the technical details of the seams on the sofa we have sat down on. It is one of her own designs. Kalarus is not just a creative but has developed a broader outlook on design, from the conception of ideas, to the technical process behind manufacturing, to marketing. Her career as a designer has followed a very fortunate path, which has afforded her the opportunity to acquire a thorough knowledge of furniture production. Trained as a product designer at the Academy of Fine Arts in Cracow, Kalarus tried her hand at advertising in 1996, before starting what turned out to be a long-lasting relationship with Polish furniture company Iker.

'I always say that Iker is where I was born as a designer,' says Kalarus. 'It was such a small company when I was working there 10 years ago. I was very fresh, without any experience. My job was to design furniture for them, but I had no knowledge of the technology, so I started to work on their PR, advertising and promotion, and doing a bit of everything. Within one year I managed to turn around the company's image. It was very interesting work because I had to challenge the owner's attitude, and convince them all about the directions to take.'

During that year Kalarus also gained an understanding about the complexity of furniture production, at which point she started to design.

'My first design was a range of sofas called Kiwi, in 2000,' recalls Kalarus. 'It was a really modern shape for the company. Before Kiwi, it had only produced furniture in black, white or yellow leather, but I convinced Iker to use fabric. I think the sofa was a stepping stone for the company. I entered it in design competitions and received a lot of media attention in Poland. The situation was very funny because the owners agreed to produce it even though it was too cutting-edge for them. The media attention it generated instantly made Iker visible on the furniture market.' As well as being a major turning point for Iker, Kiwi's innovative forms also launched Kalarus' career as a designer.

Kalarus' case is rare, however, and her encounter with Iker was fruitful, while many designers in Poland still struggle just to attract the attention of furniture producers. This is partly due to young designers' lack of knowledge about production. 'I think the problem is that you come to the factory as a designer and you don't know enough about technology. You need time to learn how it works,' says Kalarus. 'The owners of the factories have neither the

time nor the patience. But I was in a special situation: I was granted time because I did things other than design, so I was useful.'

Kalarus' confidence grew with the success of the Kiwi range and she branched out into interior design, primarily through Iker's Cracow showroom, which she ran and also designed. 'It was an interesting situation for me because I was a designer and marketing specialist, and in the shop I started to have direct contact with buyers,' says Kalarus. 'It was an excellent place to gather information. So, what do you do when there's no place for creativity? You have to decide: either I make something innovative and interesting, or I make something safe for everybody. This is something interesting for me and it has allowed me to build up my portfolio.'

In 2005 Kalarus left Iker to continue working on interior projects and collaborate with other Polish furniture companies such as Noti. 'It's going two different ways now. One way is design furniture for factories, companies and industrial companies,' explains Kalarus. 'The second way is to work in the interior design sector, designing for the residential and retail market.' The latter has proven successful for Kalarus and has led her to initiate Deko Deco, a speciality interior design store selling textiles,

wallpaper, carpets and lighting. Although Kalarus' work has gradually shifted towards the interior design industry, her furniture is still gaining attention and winning awards. One example is the Bibik Loft sofa for renowned Polish furniture company Noti, which won the Prodeco award in 2006 from Elle Decoration and more recently the Comma Chair, also for Noti, which has been awarded an honourable mention at the Red Dot Award 2009.

When asked how all these experiences in design and business had changed her, she becomes pensive. 'I think I've become a different kind of woman. I feel stronger now, more self-assured. More recently, though, a lot of my friends who are 30 or older are starting to think about family, which has made me reflect on my own choices in life. Focusing so much on my career and design, maybe I deceived myself that I have a lot of time to think about a family.'

Beata Bochińska

President of the Board, Institute of Industrial Design in Warsaw

) On my first meeting with Beata Bochińska I was impressed with the number of initiatives she manages to involve in her work at the Institute of Industrial Design in Warsaw (IWP). Her energy and direct approach to design is at times surprisingly rational and business-minded, nonetheless she is striving for Poland to achieve international recognition for its highly skilled manufacturing industry and product development.

GA One of the things that struck me about the Polish design scene was the large number of female designers. It is the opposite in the UK and the rest of Europe, where the design world seems to be male-dominated. What's your view on this?

BB There are many women in Poland involved with design projects and design-related institutions. Many of them are young designers. However, I still think that the serious designers in the industry are men. You can say the same when you visit 100% Design in London, for example, where the biggest studios are run by men.

GA That might explain why many of the Polish women designers I've met compromise working as a designer to get another job that pays the bills. Though it appears that this is also partly due to the lack of interest from Polish manufacturers to get involved with Polish designers. Why do you think this is so?

BB Actually I don't agree. I've been working with Polish manufacturers for Polish industry for more than 15 years.

Collaborating with Polish designers, we've designed more than 1,000 products. Most of them don't have a foreign brand, though, so you don't know if you are sitting on a Polish-made armchair or using a Polish-designed glass. The Polish factories are suppliers for other brands. Today in Poland there is a consistent group of 350 companies, who we keep track of and their collaborations with designers. More than 48 are working with designers. They outsource freelance designers as well as using an in-house team. Their products are more expensive than the rest of the market by about 20%-40%, but they understand that they should work with designers. All of the products they produce are Polish, but 97% of them are exported.

GA Can the remaining 3% fulfill the needs of the Polish market?

BB After 1989, everything changed in Poland with the introduction of the free market. A lot of foreign companies came to us with products which were not good enough to sell on other markets. Then the Polish producers started to export their own products because of the favourable exchange rate. Today, though, some of these companies are starting to put these on to the Polish market too, and people are surprised at the quality. The European Union [EU] is in support of this shift and is investing one billion Euros to encourage Polish companies to develop products for both global and local markets.

We have a really interesting situation with furniture and glass production in Poland: we are the third largest exporter of furniture in the world, after Germany and Italy, and we are the second largest supplier for Ikea, after China. These are the figures, we are not talking about the designers being shunned by the industry. Today I was in a meeting with a Polish producer and a Polish design studio, and they were talking about a future project to be distributed across Europe, which is going ahead thanks to the support from the European Community. We talked about quantity, mass production, prices, and how to make an innovative product. The last question was about design. And because they had this opportunity, they asked me to recommend designers.

I think the situation is divided into two parts: one is the emerging designers and the other is the core business that deals with large quantities and mass production. There is the festival for young designers in Łódź, it's very important that the designers feel they are growing together. That's their identity: "we're strong, we are a group". The second part is real life. Most Polish factories have brand new tools, having bought them between 1995 and 2005, and they all have Computer Numerical Controlled (CNC) facilities. They also have the money to afford design. When I started here two years ago, on my second day I went to the Ministry of Economy and arranged a meeting with the minister and then with some government agencies, and I started to talk about money for design. Now we have four programmes for investing in design, tools, and education for designers, project managers, and design managers.

GA Is this activity new?

BB Yes. Just a few weeks ago we started a postgraduate programme with the Business School of Economics in Warsaw, and last year I initiated a programme for design students at the University of Warsaw.

It's more complicated than just the problem between the designer and the producer or the distributor, though. We need critics, product placement, and investors. It's much easier now with EU support. We need the market. We have huge retail in Poland, so we need to provide education for designers and producers, which we've started by teaching them together how to cooperate with each other. We start with e-learning next year because a lot of factories are based outside Warsaw. It is a really huge programme, working with the Polish Producers Agency, the Ministry of Economy, the Ministry of Sciences, and the Business School of Economics.

Also, IWP was awarded a five million-Euro grant from the Polish government, financed by the EU, to establish a three-year programme supporting 550 companies and 100 design studios in Poland to improve their design management skills and share best practice. This is the biggest initiative of its kind in Poland so far, and comparable in size to similar programmes in the UK, Sweden, and Denmark.

GA So there's a synergy.

BB Absolutely. This is a great time for Poland. And actually I'm happy about the recession.

GA Why?

BB Because we have the best banking system in Europe. It's not very clever and it doesn't use many instruments so it's stable. I recently read that Poland is predicted to have the highest gross domestic product [GDP] in Europe next year. GDP is more than 5% right now and we are still growing. The situation is good for us because we know how to work at lower costs. Now all I need is wise designers.

GA What do you mean by "wise" designers?

BB I mean the difference between the stylist and the designer. We recently had the chance to put on an exhibition of Karim Rashid's work or Yves Behar. Of course they are both fantastic, but I chose Behar because he is working with non-governmental organisations [NGOs], on wide-scale democratic design: how to help people and have a real influence on their lives, and how to talk with governments about a new business model. The client is the government and the NGOs, rather than a producer or distributor, so the focus isn't on how to sell. I don't need the stylist who wants to be on the front cover of a magazine.

There are a lot of designers around the world looking at people's needs and not simply talking about sustainable or eco-design, or ergo-design. I need these kind of designers because everything else is in place. Although there are a lot of them around, they're not necessarily at the festivals because they are busy working for the companies and factories.

Companies want to cooperate with the designer as a specialist, as part of a wider process. On various occasions I've had young designers come to me asking for help with developing a good idea, and I tell them they should go to a good studio to learn the process because they have to understand how to talk with a client and how to cooperate. After five years maybe then they will be a good designer. Maybe. Poland can offer great opportunities for good designers now.

GA But what about inspiring and reconnecting people with their history?
BB Everything is changing here in Poland, museums and galleries have EU support for cultural and industrial initiatives. Not only in Warsaw, but all over the country. I think in the future there will be a lot of projects like this, we will have buildings and we will need wise and "sexy" content.

Discovering Women in Polish Design — **BEATA BOCHIŃSKA**

Anna Kotowicz–Puszkarewicz

Product designer

) Anna was the first person I interviewed for this book. Aze design, the practice she runs with Artur Puszkarewicz, is based in Czeremcha in the Podlasie region. The studio's work draws inspiration from traditional Polish crafts, and mixes poor materials with witty concepts. I remember how nervous she was before we started, but once we got talking, she had so much to say about the situation of design in Poland, it gave me the impetus to discover more.

GA How did you start your career in design?

AKP I wasn't trained as a designer: I studied history of art and then graphic design. It was a far reach to do something with design, because of my education, I only began freelancing in 2002. In Poland, art history students don't leave school with attractive career prospects. They might work in museums or art galleries but they have no opportunities to be creative and use their knowledge. The situation is very similar for graphic designers. Most of the time you are expected to know the proper software, but not to be creative and challenge the norm, and instead copy someone else's work. This is the result of the system currently in place here in Poland.

After 1989, when the free economy was instated in Poland, many private companies had to decide on their image. Their owners hired people with a grasp of the software to produce what they wanted, instead of people with their own creativity or ideas.

GA So they just want someone who will carry out the job without thinking?

AKP Yes. Because all the decisions are taken by the chief of a company, who usually knows nothing about graphics, or design in general, I turned to design. I was looking for a chance to be creative, to use my education. Working as a graphic designer is a way of earning money for me and design is a kind of big adventure, an activity where I can express myself. Every project is a new challenge. It is purely for pleasure, because we only do it for ourselves. We don't have to think about the marketing or the producer. You can be free in the creative process because there's no client to consider.

GA How long did you work as a graphic designer before you realised this?

AKP About four years. I was working in Warsaw, in a small graphics studio with private clients. This wasn't a very pleasant experience. The graphic design profession is male-dominated: women are not treated very seriously, even though that's changing now. Women tend to be treated like they're not very professional. I don't know why, it's a kind of stereotype. I'm still working as a graphic designer, however, but this is for financial reasons: design is like an expensive hobby for now.

GA It seems there are many designers in this situation in Poland. Do you think this will ever change?

AKP The situation is slowly changing already. People are interested in design but they still can't afford to buy designer items, or collect designer things. Also, there's not a serious, deep-rooted interest and understanding of the value of design, but rather a snobbery towards it.

GA Do you mean people feel it's not good enough?

AKP No, they think it's trendy, but they don't understand the different values. I don't think Polish people are ready to pay for intellectual work. They can spend their money on a flat, a car: material things that you can touch. So when I create graphics, it is difficult for people to grasp. I think it's a matter of everyday education. When Polish people see that a table can look different to how they're used to seeing it in magazines, newspapers or on television, it will be a big step for them to change the way they think about everyday things. So people will get there in small steps.

GA What's been your experience of the change from a regulated market to a free market?

AKP It's hard to say because the regime existed when I was a child and to a child everything is beautiful. Also, they don't distinguish 'needing' something or 'owning' things and wanting something.

You can see people's tastes changing. Beginning in their homes. I think if they have more examples of good design, from Italy or Spain, and all over the world, they would be more open and creative in the choices they make. On the other hand, houses and flats in Poland are very expensive and in many cases people don't have the money to furnish them. You have to eat, you have to raise a child, and give them a proper education. A beautiful table is the last thing you think about: it becomes a matter of priority, and this is a strong limitation for people.

GA So people have lost contact with their history of Polish design?

AKP Yes. People don't know or appreciate its value and history. This is a crucial problem, because our museums have good collections, but they don't have the space to exhibit them.

GA When did you realise you wanted to move away from Warsaw?

AKP I was born in Warsaw and my husband Artur only lived there for three years and we had the same feeling about living in big cities. Warsaw is a very strange city because it's hard to move around within it. There's many things that make living in Warsaw difficult, for example, it takes a long time to get from one place to another. It takes one hour to get to work and back and you must work more than eight hours. So you often work in a place with people you have nothing in common with and do a job that's not actually what you want to do. In Warsaw, there's a special kind of pressure, people are in a hurry all the time. You don't walk, you run. It's very tiring. You don't have time for you, for your personal life and your own interests.

So you live in a city but in fact you live only for your job, you are not getting anything good from the city and it becomes a kind of prison. Living that way it's easy to forget why you're doing all these things. Moving out was a risky decision because we didn't know if our studio could exist outside of Warsaw. Poland is a country with pockets of economic development.

GA Could you tell me more about the focus on craft in your work?

AKP Our interest is a result of an idealistic attitude, because we believe that design has a social responsibility. For example, by using the craft technique, you can also help disadvantaged people find some kind of part-time work by involving them in the production of their design. When you're making cigarette advertisements, for example, it's easy to forget that this promotes something that causes disease. Design has a huge responsibility.

GA Do you often return to Warsaw?

AKP You have to, even though it is possible to be outside and still stay in touch with everything that's happening in the design community and in the design market. We treat this situation as a kind of experiment. It helps us to see things clearly and more objectively.

GA How do you see the future of Polish design?

AKP Despite the past problems, I feel that the situation in Poland is constantly and dynamically changing. It's a kind of dynamic, that is quite difficult to explain to western Europe. As always, it is a complex knot of intertwined situations. The first visible change is a rapid evolution of investors, such as furniture producers. They are starting to appreciate design as a tool for answering many specific questions. I hope this is the beginning of a real change of perspective, a shift in perceiving a new reality, and not only in design.

Zuzanna Skalska

Senior consultant in design trends and insights

) Zuzanna Skalska is one of the most inspiring and energetic people I've ever come across. Even before meeting her in 2007, I had heard a lot about Skalska and her work. The next time we met was for the interview in Warsaw. Sklaska stormed in covered in snow. Clearly excited, she announced that she was to be involved in opening a new design school in Poznań, the first private design school in Poland and a milestone in the Polish education system. Later in June 2009, Skalska sent me a message saying of the project: 'this is the largest achievement in my professional life.'

GA How did you first get involved in design?

ZS I'm a second-generation Polish designer, both my parents graduated from the Academy of Fine Arts in Warsaw in 1968. My mother worked for the Institute of Industrial Design in Warsaw for 25 years and, up until 10 years ago, my father was a freelance designer. From the moment I could cut straight I was part of his one-man studio. We must have buried my grandmother a number of times: it was the excuse we used to get me out of school so I could help build things for design fairs. My parents always said I could do whatever I wanted to do in the future, so long as my job offered me freedom. Of course, they suggested being a designer. When I considered psychology, it only took a look from my father for me to know it was a bad choice.

My parents sent me money quarterly, but it wasn't enough to pay my bills, so I worked every evening in the supermarket. I wasn't a citizen of a country in the European Union [EU], so I couldn't get any financial support from Holland as a student, and I couldn't get funds from the Polish Erasmus scheme either.

GA What was your experience of the education system in The Netherlands?

ZS I started in a class for foreigners, but the three other students all spoke Dutch. During the history of art lessons I would just look at the pictures because the tutor refused to teach in English. Even more difficult was that the head of Visual Communications at the time told me it would take a while to wash my brain of the eastern European mentality. That was painful. But another teacher recommended me to the Academy of Fine Art and Design in Den Bosch.

In my third year there I lost my long-term boyfriend in a car crash. I was only 25. I was trying to make sense of life and eventually I found the answers in Witchcraft, Wicca. I also discovered a hidden Witch in me. For my graduation in 1998, I presented my vision on the world of Wicca. It consisted of 10 frames expressing typography through various materials, including handmade paper, holographic technology, screen-printing, rubber studies and resin. During my studies I did a

GA What made you move away from Poland?

ZS I went to the Academy of Fine Arts in Warsaw, but this was difficult because all of the tutors were part of the designers' network that my parents were involved in, and because of the competition, this situation made me unwelcome.

In the summer holidays, after graduation, my friend Monika and I drove her VW Passat to Holland to find work there. Arriving in Eindhoven I remember thinking: this is where I will start my higher education. It was only when I was accepted into Eindhoven Academy of Industrial Design did I think about how I was going to afford it. In Poland, schooling is free, but when I approached the Polish Ministry of Education for funding, they told me I had to pay for myself if I wanted to learn abroad. Without any support, I left Poland for The Netherlands.

At the time, my father was totally against the idea. I remember him saying to me that by going to Holland I would be leaving behind all the networks and everything they could offer me. At the same time, my mother was pushing me to take the risk, and told me not to listen to him. "Just go for it," she said. And I listened to her. It was 1992, just a few years after the Berlin Wall had come down, and Poland was readjusting economically and socially to this dramatic change.

an exceptional knowledge and experience. I then decided to move into private design consultancy. Today, after eight years of working for VanBerlo Strategy and Design, I've built up my trend expertise in a very wide scope of industrial design and I'm also responsible for the content direction of the company's 360° Trend Reports. I am also a lecturer at the Technical University in Eindhoven and a member of the board of Dutch Design Week, which brings together design, business and industry.

At the end of the Nineties I lost my Polish citizenship when I received my Dutch passport. It has helped me in my travels, but it hasn't changed the fact that my heart is still Polish. Due to my involvement in various design activities and design communities, I have hooked up with Polish companies and institutions, and met a lot of creative people, particularly in Poznań.

GA What is your involvement with Poznań?
ZS It's the capital of the Wielkopolska, which is a partner of the North Brabant, where I live in The Netherlands. They were once both rich and industry-led regions. I feel like I've met the right kind of people there who understand the power of innovation and design, and Wielkopolska is the perfect starting point for design as part of the future strategy of the region.

six-month internship in the New Business and Special Projects department of Philips Electronics. My dream was to work for Philips' creative department.

After my graduation I applied and miraculously got an interview with Philips Design's senior vice-president at the time, Peter Nagelkerke. He was amazed with my work and said: 'wow, a witch! We have to have her in our design team.' Peter gave me a rather futuristic-sounding position as Sensorial Trend Analyst.

GA What did that entail?
ZS I worked in the Ambient Intelligence department. Ten years ago we weren't ready to understand what this entails because rather than touch-based interaction, Ambient Intelligence relies on tech sensors. I worked in the Strategic Design Department on future concepts and trends and the most important tendency was, and still is, that our environment is getting more intelligent. Due to the miniaturization of technology, products are getting smaller, simpler and are increasingly sensorial. Working in this department I started to understand that this is a totally different way of intending design. It is not what will come tomorrow, but what will come the day after tomorrow.

After more than two years working for Philips, I had built up

And now I am involved with Li Edelkoort in the creation of the first dedicated school of design, for 300 students. This beautiful idea was only possible due to two fantastic people and true believers: Piotr Voelkel, owner of Meble VOX Company, who also owns The School of Humanities and Journalism in Poznań and Lech Wojtasiak, vice marshal of Wielkopolska.

Piotr bought a historic printing house that is situated in the centre of Poznań. This early-20th century building has already become a legendary place in the city. His dream is to open the Design Centre of Wielkopolska, as a place where design, innovative ideas and business come together. Our design school will be part of this project. It will be funded by the EU, the Polish government, Wielkopolska and Poznań. The future belongs to those who believe in dreams. I am an optimist, and I believe that good things will happen.

GA So Polish design will finally be put on the map?

ZS I think Polish design is already on the map, but not on the European map. For me, because I'm an outsider, Poland has a clear net. For example, Łódź is more about graphic design and photography; Cracow focuses on product design: manufacturing with a Bohemian touch; Silesia is about craft: the forgotten tradition and techniques, and then there's Gdańsk, which is about nautical design. Something is definitely cooking in the Polish design scene. I think that the biggest secret about design in other parts of Europe is the absence of a central system. All regional centres communicate, which creates a chain of cooperation that gives design a stronger position as a national product. In Poland we still lack an understanding about the role of design management.

In the Nineties, western Europe defined what design means and everybody understood they could earn money by investing in it. It changed the definition from design as a shape-making process, to be seen as added value and business. Now they understand that design is changing companies, on every level, and that design should play a role. Design is like a central platform for a company structure: and this is what they call design management. Western Europe understands that you can put design and design management on different levels. Poland is just discovering and beginning to understand design now. This is the moment when the mentality will also have to change. The first wind of change came in the Nineties and now the second will come along with global financial crisis.

GA Sometimes it takes a person from outside to understand this, and see the whole picture.

ZS I am an outsider, but I speak the same language. That makes me powerful. Don't forget that in Poland we don't have time for evolution as a means of developing. Europe has already had 30 years of evolution. While in Poland, everything is squashed in. There's no time left. In some ways it's working well, some places never had the time to develop design, and they just buy it.

For me, Poland has a very Mediterranean mentality, with a "mañana" attitude. What also made us is our religion.

I grew up as a Catholic, then I landed in a Protestant country. Somehow, mentally I became a Protestant. I am finding happiness and satisfaction in my job, and I respect God in everything I do. Whereas in Poland, people don't really find their jobs enjoyable. The Polish education system creates artists. You are either an artist or an engineer in Poland, there is nothing in-between.

GA What do you think will happen next?

ZS People are thinking: if I'm not an artist, I'm a designer; I also make pictures and design a magazine. Everyone's now putting everything under a design umbrella, which is OK if you understand design, but if you don't it's like you're fighting. We have to approach design in the way we are going to approach the future.

In 2006, the first wave of immigration students started to come back. I hope people with PhDs and MAs will come back too. This is why we are initiating things here, we hope that these people from abroad will come over and speak fluent English and bring connections to Poland.

GA This situation is so particular to Poland whereby the more people that come back, the wealthier the design community becomes with different points of view and new approaches.

ZS This is what we need in Poland: a wide and strong

Ela Skrzypek + Magda Małczyńska-Umeda

Designers

) A stork landing on its nest is the simple yet incisive concept that Studio Bakalie has developed for the recent campaign: 'have you got a PLan to return?' commissioned by the Polish government. The financial downturn in the last year has significantly weakened the pound sterling against other currencies, including the Euro. As a direct consequence, many Poles, who originally fled to the UK when Poland joined the European Union in 2004, are now migrating back to their own country.

As part of the campaign, Bakalie has created a short film, website and booklets. 'The aim of this campaign is to anticipate the questions people are most likely to ask in preparation for returning to Poland,' explains Ela Skrzypek, co-founder of the practice. 'The campaign has to capture a very large audience and social strata of Poles.'

Studio Bakalie has managed to infuse some humour into the campaign and inserted some less obvious questions: 'is four kilos of strawberries already smuggling?' With its red-and-white colour-coded animation echoing the colours of the Polish flag, and overlaid with a composition by Chopin, it is also a nod to a nationalistic spirit. While noticing this, I also realise the meeting room we are sat in is a reference to the Polish flag, with white walls and red chairs (not an intentional association, they explain to me later). Only a grey polystyrene chair breaks the pattern: it is one of the 500 that was given away by Tom Dixon in Trafalgar

Square during the 2006 London Design Festival, which Skrzypek carried back with her.

The Bakalie studio is in an ex-military complex in Warsaw. They were among the first to rediscover the block, which was built in the 19th century and is now mostly occupied by creative practices. Skrzypek and Małczyńska-Umeda set up Bakalie in 2000 after graduating in graphic design from the Academy of Fine Arts in Warsaw in the same year. Skrzypek also studied brand management at the School of Economics in Warsaw in 2007, and Małczyńska-Umeda completed her postgraduate studies in management in 2008 at the same school. 'The tools we work with are visual: we both feel that one picture means a thousand words,' says Skrzypek. 'Sometimes it is much easier to communicate the different values and description of a brand in pictures.'

The use of direct visual references is characteristic of Studio Bakalie's ethos: reliant on quality and simplicity and clear communication. What it produces is bespoke branding, so it invests time in clients and always tries to work closely with them on projects. Indeed, the studio runs workshops with its clients to inform its research. 'The ingredients of our work are primarily Polish, this is not necessarily our philosophy, it is just the way things are. We have an appreciation of Polish aesthetics, which has its roots in Polish graphic design from the 1920s and 1960s,' says Skrzypek. 'We have witnessed the dramatic cultural change that has happened

Ela Skrzypek

— Without creating nostalgic imagery or products, Studio Bakalie's work is helping to reinforce a sense of national identity and pride —

Magda Małczyńska-Umeda

since the end of the Communist regime, and the move into the free market.'

Poland is still undergoing this process of economic transformation. In the early Nineties, though, in the fast switch-over to the free market, Polish professionals found themselves completely unprepared due to the lack of structures in place to respond to these shift. The end result was an overall state of confusion, which is still evident in the design and branding spheres. 'We are still trying to establish a common platform for all of us in the field,' Skrzypek says enthusiastically. 'The market is changing so fast in Poland, it's offering challenges and opportunities, so it's extremely exciting for us. It's the reason why I've chosen to stay in Poland.'

Studio Bakalie are at the forefront of these shifts in the industry: instigating changes through being pro-active and involved. Skrzypek and Małczyńska-Umeda are the co-founders and active members of the Association of Emerging Designers and of the Brand Design Club (which Skrzypek also chairs), both helping Polish designers and branding experts to share best practice in the creative industry. In 2001, after setting up the studio, Skrzypek lived and worked in Italy for two years. 'It was like looking into the future,' she says. 'I learnt as much as I could from a more developed market and brought it back here to Poland.'

Studio Bakalie's ability to reinterpret something very Polish with a witty and refreshing approach makes it a popular choice particularly for public projects, including a commission in 2005 by the Polish Post (Poczta Polska) to design the picture on four different-priced stamps. For this project, Studio Bakalie took inspiration from traditional Polish embroidery. 'We had red roses embroidered and photographed,' says Skrzypek. 'I'm a big fan of Polish art and craft, and this was a great project because it gave us the opportunity to use a traditional Polish craft in a contemporary context.'

Studio Bakalie has a unique approach to graphic design. Communication is an integral part of the tumultuous and exciting time Polish design is experiencing, and the studio's ability to draw inspiration from the country's heritage, without creating redundant or nostalgic imagery or products is helping to reinforce a sense of national identity and pride. 'My grandfather died fighting, he sacrificed his life for the future of his country,' says Skrzypek. 'Sometimes I feel his strength is in me and the work I do: I feel the common interest among my own people and the will to improve our future. This might sound over the top, but there is truth in it.'

Agata Kulik-Pomorska
Product designer

) Agata Kulik-Pomorska is one of those special people who possesses an inner calm. The day we met for the interview we also had the television crew from Domo filming us for a pilot of its documentary on Polish women designers. While I was agitated by their presence, Kulik-Pomorska patiently sat on the sofa. Although our conversation was focused on the work she does with her husband Paweł Pomorski at their design practice Malafor, what emerged was her positive vision and the trust she has in the future of Polish design.

GA How did you get involved in design?

AKP I studied interior architecture at the Academy of Fine Arts in Gdańsk. When I graduated in 2003 my final project won The President of the Republic of Poland Grand Prix and that paved my way into the design world. The prize was an exhibition in Królikarnia gallery, which is a part of the National Musuem in Warsaw. I was given one year to prepare for the exhibition and this was a real challenge because I had 100sq m available, but didn't have anything to show as I had just started my career as a designer. So, together with my husband Pawel, we founded Malafor and started to create pieces for the exhibition. The gallery walls were very tall, so we designed a two metre-high seat-cum-ladder, for people to sit and see the world below from a different perspective.

GA What did you do after the exhibition, after the hype and attention it generated?

AKP It wasn't so easy, as we had to start thinking about money and the commercial aspects of Malafor. My ambition has always been to work as a designer and I didn't want to compromise that. We started producing designs ourselves: we had tried to establish some contacts with manufacturers when we started out, but it was very difficult to find someone who wanted to produce our designs.

GA This is a problem many of your colleagues are having here in Poland.

AKP Manufacturers don't do small productions, it is a setback, and investment is hard to come by if you have limited editions or designs. The manufacturers we talked to were only interested in producing work on a large scale, but our designs are not for mass production.

There's always a great need for big investment to create a prototype, and for clear communication between manufacturer and designer.

GA How do you think this could be improved?

AKP It is important that they both understand and respect each other's point of view. The situation is evolving very fast here in Poland, though, and we are only at the beginning. It is a really good time for studios like ours, which are taking the first steps toward mass production.

GA Your designs are always so finely detailed and finished. How do you decide on the materials you use?

AKP We want to design furniture that's very simple and easily made. We tend to take readily available materials and use them in a different way. So most of the time we design in relation to what we find already in production. For example, we used PVC drainpipes to make a storage system. We painted them and stacked them to form either a storage space, or a partition.

GA Your work also draws inspiration from nature.

AKP Yes, we created a stool that mixed nature with artificial materials. It consisted of a log wrapped in a sheet of shiny, stainless steel. At the Łódź Design Festival in 2008, we presented a suspended speaker, Bolo

Acoustic Man. The inspiration for that was the formation of foam and the intersections between multiplying bubbles. And my friend Paweł Olejniczak specially composed a score of minimalistic music for the piece.

GA It is interesting that Polish designers are keen to mix traditional crafts with new technologies and materials.

AKP In Poland, we tend to take a lot of inspiration from traditions and folklore. It's only recently that we've had a chance to deliver it in a contemporary way. This is also about trying to find our own identity and language through design, rather than copying it from abroad. Often the questions are posed: what is Polish design? And what does it look like? So maybe we are looking for the answers. We have a great history of design from the late 1940s to the 1960s, when it wasn't really in the mind of the consumers because it wasn't available to them. Not many Poles know about these Polish design traditions.

GA This is a complex operation of communication to reconnect Poles to their own design heritage.

AKP Often in my research I've come across Polish design from the Fifties or Sixties, but such discoveries have been almost by accident, and only after completing my education. The history of Polish design is simply not part of the curriculum, even though we learnt a lot about design in other countries.

GA What makes you stay in Poland?

AKP Things are moving fast here, possibly faster than the rest of Europe. But Poland is still catching up, despite the recent economic downturn. So as a designer you also have to catch up very quickly, you have to understand things and process things at a phenomenal pace. Some designers have been doing this by gaining experience abroad, somewhere in Europe or the US, and coming back to offer a different perspective. Personally, I have never thought about going abroad. I want to stay and work in Poland, I feel good here.

Teresa Kruszewska

Interior designer

) I met Professor Teresa Kruszewska in Warsaw in the winter of 2008. When I arrived for the interview, Kruszewska was winding up a previous meeting. The table was crowded with maquettes made of balsa wood, drawings, and an arch-lever folder spread open containing black-and-white photographs of furniture and construction details. Although we were in a cafe, it felt like being in Kruszewska's studio and entering into her world.

Some of the small models of children's furniture and pedagogic games recalled in their forms a purity and functionality typical of Scandinavian design. In her professional life, Kruszewska has dedicated most of her energy to children's furniture. I later found out that wonderful prototypes she had showed me during our interview are now part of the National Museum in Poland, and are displayed in exhibitions in Poland and abroad.

This made me feel particularly privileged to be have seen and held these original, beautifully crafted designs.

Leafing through the thick files, Kruszewska's passion and her attention to detail became apparent as she paused at every page to comment on the drawings. Kruszewska speaks fluent English having learnt it as a child. This skill has opened many doors in her career: allowing her to travel as a young designer to Scandinavia and the US, even when Poland was still behind the Iron Curtain of the Communist Bloc.

Between 1959 and 1963, Kruszewska worked intensely on the development of the furniture for the Pediatric Institute of the Medical Academy of Cracow (now the Pediatric Hospital in Cracow-Prokocim). The facility was built and equipped thanks to donations from the US government, the American foundation Project Hope, and funds gathered among Polish diaspora in the US and Canada. 'I designed flexible furniture for the Medical Academy to go in a lounge room where children could rest and have their meals,' says Kruszewska. 'I designed a single stool that could be adapted for different heights and used by all children, simply turning it upside down.'

Kruszewska had the furniture built by Mebloartyzm, a small furniture cooperative in Wojnicz near Cracow. 'The only difficulty was that the cooperative had previously never produced plywood furniture,' says Kruszewska. 'However, workers were very quick to learn the new technology. I found this very young, clever man, and together we started to design some new forms to challenge the bentwood technique.'

In 1963, thanks again to her grasp of English, a tutor at the Academy of Fine Arts in Warsaw put Kruszewska's name forward for a scholarship in Finland, where she then trained at Alvar Aalto's studio. In 1966 Kruszewska received a one-year scholarship to the US where she gathered experiences in different fields, from design, to photography and art. 'When I went out to the US, the Vietnam War was raging,' she says. 'I was taken as a postgraduate student on this scholarship. It was very hard to begin with, because in Warsaw I was helped by the assistants and the machine operators: I only drew the projects and passed them on to the technicians. In the US, however, I had to do everything myself and they watched me very carefully to see how this woman from a Communist country had come to be there, so I wanted to show them that I could do it. It wasn't easy, but I tried my best.'

In America, Kruszewska studied at the Rhode Island School of Design in Providence. The equipment and facilities at the school were of a standard that Kruszewska hadn't experienced in Poland, so she started working designing furniture and eventually tried her hand at making jewellery, and photography. 'Working on some furniture design while in the US I learnt how to do vacuum mouldings,' says Kruszewska. 'I didn't realise how dangerous this machine was, but I started to learn how to use it. I learnt how to make very thin, strong pieces by layering and gluing the material in different directions.'

After one year abroad, Kruszewska returned to Poland in 1967 with an ambition to improve the quality of children's furniture in her own country. With an opportunity to travel in order to inform her research into the subject,

she visited Norway, Germany and Finland.
'I wanted to improve kindergartens in Poland,' she says.
'Because women had to work and we were lacking in
good conditions to care for children. I designed some
equipment for kindergartens and some for private
homes.' Kruszewska's working method and ethos
throughout her career has been relentless trials and
testing until the product has felt right for the designer
and the user.

'The most important aspect of my work is that I always test
with children and with grown-ups,' she explains. 'All
my products are based on ergonomics. This is a rule
design students should always follow: to base, and test
their designs on real life.' Throughout her professional
career as a designer, Kruszewska has approached design
solutions in a very pragmatic yet intuitive way. Despite

the fulfillment she has experienced from her career, one
can sense a certain sadness in Kruszewska's words that
she has not seen her designs through to production. 'I
am very happy that I've had all these experiences,' she
explains. 'But I also feel like a revolutionary who fights
and fights without any results.'

Having worked with poor materials such as plywood and string,
Kruszewska has come from a background where materiality
challenges were much more pertinent, yet she has always focused
on the end-user rather than the aesthetic. A crucial and functional
approach has been partially lost in design education, as students
are more keen to explore the extent to which computer software
can calculate conditions for a specific furniture design. 'I'm very
glad my designs are still relevant prototypes that I can show
students and help them understand how they can physically,
rather than virtually, tackle design issues.'

Anna Wojczyńska
Interior designer

) I met Anna Wojczyńska in her and Wojciech Wachowski's showroom Zoom, a vast 1,200sq m space in the heart of Warsaw. The meeting room where we sat for our interview has been strategically positioned on the first floor overlooking the landscape of design furniture. Zoom feels like a wonderland. Its sequence of meandering spaces entreats visitors to search and discover. It is also a very special place for design, particularly for students as they can view and touch the latest products coming out of the best furniture companies around the world.

GA How did you find a place like this right in the centre of Warsaw?

AW We've been here for about 10 years. We found it because we had been to Milan and I thought, I can't show in a small existing showroom, so we put out an advertisement looking for a large space. Someone responded and when we came to view it we were immediately taken by the sheer scale of it. There aren't many industrial places like this left in Warsaw, especially not in the centre, and the ones outside are too far out. There used to be many more, but most of them have gone to make space for new developments. Mostly housing. In the centre you can probably find about 400sq m spaces, but nothing like this.

We have the showroom downstairs and one level is occupied by Vis-à-Vis, our interior design company, which we started in 1989. The space is so vast, we have a lot of things that even our staff don't know are on the shelves.

GA What type of projects does Vis-à-Vis do?

AW It depends. Mainly we do private residences, because then we can have a better budget. We work across Poland, we also have projects in Moscow, the US and recently in Berlin. We have a very limited group of customers, we don't advertise for Vis-à-Vis, its all by word of mouth. Also, it's difficult working here in Poland. When I look at foreign design magazines such as Frame, for example, I notice that there is a big gap between what we can do here and what is happening abroad. There is a big difference in taste and money.

GA How long have you been running the showroom?

AW Altogether we've been in this business for about 20 years. It's funny because my first projects were done in the time when you were not able to buy tiles, or glue for the tiles. There was a special shop where you could buy luxury products: Coca-Cola, chewing gum, peanuts and so on. All from abroad. But you couldn't buy 30m of tiles. You couldn't do a normal project. And when we wanted to call companies abroad to get catalogues, or to talk to firms, all international calls were blocked, so you'd have to call a special lady to say: "I want to have a connection with France." And she would say: "OK, this will be a two hour wait". In Communist times you

couldn't have direct contact with the West. There were no mobiles back then.

GA Has it been hard to gain the confidence of brands such as Moooi to give you pieces for your showroom?

AW I was working with Moooi and Tom Dixon before people knew who they were. For example, we had been ordering Moooi products way before its connection with B&B Italia. We are now in the position whereby companies are asking to be shown at Zoom.

GA Do you also produce your own lighting?

AW Yes. When we designed the lamps, we had a terrible problem finding producers. There were either very poor producers with no machines and no knowledge, or ones which were really good, but weren't interested in producing for a Polish company, because the were working with Danish or German organisations.

GA What do you think about the relationship between the local manufacturers and local designers in Poland?

AW It's a disaster, a closed circle. The public is not ready for the things that would be acceptable outside Poland. So the manufacturers want to produce things that can easily be sold in Poland. The education system is also responsible for this situation.

Discovering Women in Polish Design — **ANNA WOJCZYŃSKA**

GA Why?

AW Mainly it's because of the staff. They are too old, with no experience and no knowledge about the changes that Polish design is going through and what is really going on in terms of design around the world. We do get people bringing their portfolios to us, and their projects are really good but they don't realise that these things already exist, or are already on the market, sometimes they just show copies. So they're not pushing the boundaries to create something new. In product design its a bit better, but interior design is a disaster!

GA Are the good Polish manufacturers concentrating on producing foreign design?

AW I don't know when this will change. It's partly Polish people's mentality and their taste, which is changing a little bit. This is that strange time when you have to wait and see what happens. Quite often I want to show something and I'm really enthusiastic about it and love it, but I have to consider whether people will understand it and rethink whether I really want to show it. I'm in a strange position because this also has to work from a financial perspective. I can't do what I'd love to do as I also have to calculate the risk. This is really frustrating when you find something and it's really fantastic and you have to wait until people catch on to the idea. For example, we are showing some pieces by the Campana brothers, and we can see from the Internet that a lot of people are looking at it but are afraid to buy it. So at Zoom we're pushing a little bit with strange new products, showing some things that people aren't sure how to react to. It's the philosophy of your space: you decide which customer is interesting to you and that informs your products and how you show them.

Well, it's the general strategy of Zoom: some people are disappointed it's not luxurious here, but generally people are afraid of money, design and anything expensive. So I decided not to do it in an exclusive way because a lot of people would never come here. On the other hand, for others it's still too exclusive. The first thing they check is the prices. If they think they can afford it they are not afraid. We also want to teach people that it's not my idea how much the sofa costs, but that it's a normal price for furniture. People think it's one zero too much, but they've never had a chance to learn about prices. Often they are so shocked they think we're joking. Once we displayed in store, and put online, a leather hammock designed by Patricia Urquiola. It's a very expensive item. I checked on the blogs and people were commenting on the price, they were shocked. Nobody was buying it, but they were all talking about it.

80

Katarzyna Okińczyc

Product designer

) When I met Katarzyna Okińczyc in October 2007, she had just got back from Chicago. I'll never forget the day we had the interview for the book, it was a deep winter's day, and Okińczyc had travelled from Poznań in the middle of the night to get to Warsaw to meet me. We met at the 3F showroom, and the TV channel Domo was filming us for its documentary on Polish women designers. It was the first time we had been filmed, and although it took some time, eventually we relaxed and were able to talk in depth about Okińczyc's experience of working in America and her ambitions on returning to Poland.

GA Why did you leave Poland to go to America in the first place?

KO I left because there weren't enough opportunities back then in Poland and I wanted to do something that was bigger and better and that would matter. I decided to do something that would give me skills and equip me with a commercial approach. I spent four years in Berlin where the people are arty and cool, but I found there still wasn't enough industrial skill behind any of it to fully meet my expectations. You see cool ideas but they're not real products. Whereas the process in America appeared to be really professional.

GA Could you tell me more about your experience of living and working there?

KO I travelled around a lot. I was in Boston first and then Chicago. As far as design offices are concerned, the companies aren't as interesting as those in San Francisco or New York, but they are reasonable, they don't do over the top stuff, which is

81

good if you want to learn solid skills. During the stay I worked for two different consultancies doing new product concepts for Proctor and Gamble. It was good, but not very ethical because of the polymers, and chemicals involved. I was really good at that but I still wanted to gain a more hands-on experience in the developing process and engineering, so I moved to another, more engineering-based company in Chicago. It turned out I wouldn't have been able to do this job for too long because you can't really bring your own concepts to the table. It's all given to you from the engineers, but it was really exciting, and I learnt how to develop various products.

GA Why did you decide to come back? Did you feel like you had achieved your goals in America?

KO Well, you can never really learn enough, but my visa was for two years, so if I wanted to stay I would have been obliged to stay with the same company for five years and it seemed like too much of a commitment at the time. America is amazing, the culture is so open. Once you have understood how it works, and why it works the way it does, youjust embrace it. From a European perspective it seems really commercial and without roots, but once you get rid of that prejudice you start to feel like you're part of it.

By this stage, I had been out of Poland for six years altogether and I hadn't had time to think in-between coming back from Berlin and going to America, so I wanted to see how things were back at home. This is something that matters more: contributing to the place I'm from. At first my Polish was terrible, because I don't really like reading or writing. If you're a foreigner you don't care too much about having a grasp of the language, but in your own country, where you used to be a clever person but you can't even write business letters, it was extremely frustrating. So I spent the first six months acclimatising. My idea was to come back to Poland and look for opportunities doing things that would put me on the design map here. I have skills but what's the use if no one knows about me? This is especially true in Europe: I get the impression that it's more about whether you've been exhibited in a gallery, or published in a magazine. I think in America they believe more in skill than being the flavour of the month. On the other hand, most of the designers over there remain anonymous for their whole careers and that's probably not ideal either.

GA For your most recent project you have worked with crystal, which is a very traditional material in Poland. Is this process of rethinking Polish traditions and crafts a way to reconnect with a wide audience?

KO Yes. But even the people who work with crystal think there's no future in it. It was very hard to convince them to work with us. They think no one wants them anymore and that they've been forgotten. A good example is a guy making his living from crystal cutting and ornamenting, when we met him he was quite depressed, and now he's in a magazine it's like he's suddenly high-tech. It's great.

You need to embrace the new to come back to the old, to think freely about your past. That's what's happening right now. People are ready for change because their reflecting on the past, and for a long time people that wasn't spoken about. They wanted to erase everything. I was worried about Poland in terms of culture because we live in this era whereby information comes through so fast. All the trends, technology, and culture is coming and going so fast, and we still haven't figured out what our own traditions are. There is no time to get our own culture back on track because so much stuff is bombarding us from outside. I'm happy at this point, though: there is room to be objective.

GA And what is your view on the innovation in materials and technology in Poland?

KO I think there is new stuff out here, but it is not really sustaining itself. The inventors often don't yet realise they should be commercial, so if you get to them in time you might come out with a really good product. For me as a designer, innovation is the key. Even with this crystal project, I want to do something that's functional and solves a problem. I don't just want to make nice shapes. Design is about discovering new things and trying to go with the flow of society: creating the future.

I try to be innovative in what I do, for example, with the 60 Bag, which is entirely developed and manufactured in Poland. The bag is non-woven flax fabric, it's made out of industrial waste during flax processing. And once you throw the bag away it actually disappears after 60 days.

GA How did you come across this material for the 60 Bag?

KO It's a really exciting project. I'm trying to work with different people to get the best results. I started working with a photographer, Remigiusz Truchanowicz, and also a brand specialist. He got in touch with an institute of natural fibres, in Poznań, which houses these amazing materials. He brought some back and we chose this as being the best for a short-term, relatively low-cost, commercial, but innovative project. So we took the material and several designs, made

the website and came up with a strategy, that's how I like to work: create the whole package. We're cooperating with the Institute of Industrial Design in Warsaw and working together on the commercialisation of their inventions. Right now we only have samples, but we've started meeting with retailers, so that they exchange plastic bags for these ones or simply sell them off the shelf. I'm trying to start with the high-end market because they're not as cheap as plastic bags. But it's all manufactured in Poland, everything is developed and sold here. I really wanted to do a green product that looks hip, so it's perceived as a high-end product, not 'for the sake of the world lets sacrifice style'.

GA How have you found fitting back into the Polish design community?

KO I had friends who still remembered me, so I was able to make some money. I've been researching what's out there: the identity, the patriotism of Poland: what's interesting in our history that people don't really appreciate, but they love in the end because they rediscover things that they're nostalgic about. I won the Prodeco award this year with Elle Decoration Poland. I was really surprised because I never thought they would award it to an independent designer. It was for Cabo[b] released under the label Dogenvol. It's a globe in cut crystal, which contains cables for USBs. It's re-interpreting history in a modern way, which gets people really excited, and that was the plan. To get some attention.

Anna Siedlecka

Product designer and lighting manufacturer

) At first, Anna Siedlecka strikes me as a very quiet person, but the more we talked the more her incredible energy and passion for design was revealed. Siedlecka's obsession with light has led her to build a business around it, from its design, to production and distribution. She set up Puff-Buff studio with her partner, Rodek Achramowicz, and developed it into a company that now distributes in 20 countries. What transpired during our conversation was an inspiring message to all designers starting out, an open invitation to take courage and get on with it.

GA When did you start up your lighting company?

AS Puff-Buff was set up in 2004, although I was working as a freelance designer beforehand. I finished my studies in 2002, and the studio and the projects have been growing ever since. We have also shown our products in Milan and other design fairs around the world. To begin with we were exhibiting just to gauge a response, but then people wanted to buy the lighting so we had to set up the production side too. It's growing really fast.

GA This has been a good move for your company then?

AS Yes, but not an easy one. When you're the producer you have to think about the marketing, sales and distribution.

We had to learn how to do it all because we were normal working people. At the start, we had no idea how to work with agents, nor about production. But over time, having made many mistakes along the way, we have learnt how to do all of this. Now we're growing, we can hire more people, because **a**t the moment we're a family business with a few accountants, electricians, collaborating with a few agencies, and people who create our advertising.

GA Your inflatable lighting is unique: there isn't an obvious connection between electricity, lighting and this plastic.

AS Yes, it's a strange combination that always attracts a lot of curiosity. Inflatable structures have great potential: they can be very big yet lightweight. The fact that it can be deflated and shrink to a fraction of its inflated size means it is easily transportable and cost effective. For exhibitions in Paris and Milan we carried all our products in rucksacks on our backs. All we needed to do was pump them up and plug them in.

GA Why have you chosen bubble forms in particular?

AS I like designs from the Fifties: I like rounded shapes. Also, we wanted to design something funny, we didn't want to design very serious things. You can kick our chandelier, and it can fall on your head nothing will happen. We invented it while we were on holiday. People were selling

big inflatable beach balls near to the beach, and we thought, we must do a lamp like this.

GA Before Puff-Buff, you worked as a shoe designer. Do you miss working in that sector?

AS Yes. Fashion was something I liked, but I don't feel like a fashion designer. The shoe designing was an adventure. It wasn't the kind of shoes I wanted to do, so I got bored. I wanted to do something more industrial and they wanted me to do something more casual.

Light is my obsession. I love to create light and I have strong desire to do that. And I know how it works. It fulfills a certain fascination. It's the same with inflatable design, its also something I can't stop doing! Sometimes I think I'd like to do something different but I'm too deep in it and I can't start something else!

GA You've been very brave to set up a new design business. It seems that many Polish designers are too afraid to do it.

AS At first we had no money and no time, we didn't know how to start. We too were afraid to invest in it and leave our jobs. You have to be able to support yourself, so I understand other designers' worries, but I think you must also take risks and make moves. We're always saying to young designers here that they should start to produce their designs, start to do something, show ideas at a fair, or wherever. But they all reply: "I would like to but no, no, you know how it is." I just wish they'd be more brave.

GA As well as taking risks, you also need to see how people respond to your design. Otherwise how can you progress?

AS Exactly. You must show it and you must produce it. Take some action. But people are afraid. It was hard to make the first move. I was lucky because my parents helped to financially support me. At the time, we were also doing an interior design project and the money from that went into the design company. It's worth taking the risk. If you believe and if you want do it, make it it happen.

GA Some Polish designers are complaining that there is good design but no investment from local manufacturers.

AS Yes, you can complain but you must also do something about it. I think one outcome of the Communist era is that we've learnt to carry on somehow. So when you don't have good materials, you must paint it, or you must sew your clothes. You must learn how to make something from nothing. When I finished my studies I didn't know about the business side of design, we weren't taught that at school. However, now we've learnt it ourselves, and we keep learning all the time with each new project.

GA Are you able to pass on the knowledge you have acquired running Puff-Buff to younger generations of designers?

AS Myself and my partner Radek Achramowicz are often invited to present lectures on our work at the design departments of Polish academies and universities. We usually talk about designing but most people are interested in marketing. They know how to design, they want to know the practicalities: how to produce it; sell it; how and where to show it, and how much money to charge. We are trying to teach young people all of this and also tell them: "don't be afraid, just do it."

Marta Rowińska

Designer

) Marta Rowińska's work is continuously challenging the idea of scale, whether it's a handbag or a building. Trained in architecture at the Technical University in Warsaw, she went on to study textiles and fashion at the Academy of Fine Arts in Łódź. The following year, in 2007, she set up the multidisciplinary studio Beton with architect Lech Rowiński.

Our meeting took place in Rowińska's flat in Warsaw, which doubles as a studio. It is located on the second floor of an austere residential block, reminiscent of the architecture of Austrian master Adolf Loos. Her clothes look like her own design: fluid, baggy trousers resting on her hips below a plain T-shirt. She spoke softly when explaining her projects. An equally soft rain fell outside and although it was mid-morning, the photographer had to use a flash to compensate for the lack of sunlight.

Looking around Rowińska's studio it was clear that her interest lies in modularity: a gridded artwork, which she has used as a starting point for Beton's website, and a geometric felt handbag, a project, which she has been working on for some time, trying to find the most accurate technical solutions. 'Sometimes you have to leave the project to one side,' she explains picking up the item. 'Even temporarily forget about it, to be able to discover it again and see it in a different perspective.'

Besides the ongoing issues with the technicalities of her new fashion accessory, Rowińska has been involved in a recently completed architecture project. 'It is a private commission for a small rural church in the village of Tarnów, overlooking the biggest Polish river, the Vistula,' says Rowińska. The building is constructed entirely out of wood, with a shingle-style roof, which seamlessly transforms into the side walls. 'In architecture, as in textile design, you can work with texture, you can design the system to achieve that, as is the case with the wooden elements for Tarnów's church.' explains Rowińska. The back wall of the church, behind the altar, is made of glass and opens up the view to a distant horizon. The repetition of the delicate shingle modules on the roof and facade are uneven, giving the whole building an organic texture, which makes it special.

'We design architecture, when we are sure we can do
something of certain quality,' says Rowińska. 'Since 1989
there has been a big construction boom in Poland. There
are too many site developers looking for architects to
simply shape the space and squeeze the most out of
it. The quality of the space is worth close to nothing.
That's not the work for us. We are perfectly happy with
less projects, taking on only those we're comfortable
with.' Rowińska's interest in modularity and duplication
manifests itself more clearly and organically when
applied to fabric and textiles than in her architectural
projects, as she fuses the rigid geometry of a modular
structure with the softness of the fabrics she selects.
Indeed, her fashion work has a purity, which brings to
mind the work of the Japanese fashion designer Issey
Miyake, the T-cloud is a case in point.

'Apparently the T-cloud looks like a pleated jacket and
appears soft,' she says stretching the folds. 'Structurally,
though, the jacket is composed of three layers of different
fabrics sewn together, which gives it certain sculptural
qualities: it has a softness, stiffness and flexibility at the
same time.' Rowińska approaches fashion collections the
same as she does her architecture projects, in that they
are very unique and not dictated by the industry. 'We are

Discovering Women in Polish Design — **MARTA ROWIŃSKA**

— We apply the same approach to fashion and furniture as we do to architecture: they use different tools but require the same thinking. It is all design —

not big producers. We make only limited editions and relatively small items,' says Rowińska. 'So that way I have the freedom to do what I want and also to create things specifically for clients or friends. In reality there are no divisions between fashion, architecture, or graphics. The tools are different, but the process of thinking, of defining answers for certain questions is the same. It is all design.'

Rowińska has also been working on costumes for dance performances for choreographers such as Rodney Place; the collective, Universal Law of Impermanence with Kaya Kołodziejczyk, and Bretoncaffe Theatre. In some cases she has developed the actual stage design as in Queen Lizard Manifesto, which she designed with Rowiński in 2007 for Bretoncaffe, the Polish dance theatre. 'For Bretoncaffe we created a modular wall structure using interlocking triangular cardboard elements,' says Rowińska. 'We are now trying to develop this concept into an architectural system, which we could use in shaping interiors, and possibly exteriors, of buildings.'

Rowińska's experience in various design fields lets her see everything with a fresh perspective. Architectural considerations ooze into fashion design, and equally, her sensitivity toward fabric and texture affects how she thinks about large-scale projects. 'They're similar: you feel that there's architecture somewhere in textile design and the other way around,' she tells me. 'Architecture is very complex in terms of programming and thinking, you can create a variety of other things by applying the same approach.'

Rowińska has an ability to think laterally and apply her understanding of architecture to various sized projects. She compares it to unlocking a mechanism. 'Somehow, like a system or a set of modular elements, once you've understood one piece, you can replicate it. That's what I do. I find it particularly inspiring to work across more than one area of design. Somehow they all inform each other and help me to develop my thinking process and new ideas.'

Monika Ostaszewska + Zofia Konarska + Klementyna Jankiewicz

Product designers

) The creativity that sparks off Monika Ostaszewska, Zofia Konarska and Klementyna Jankiewicz is infectious. The three women form design studio Baba Akcja, an international design outfit working from two countries. The studio is prolific as projects are usually conceived in a short period of time and completed very quickly, hot on the heels of the next.

We met in a cafe in central Warsaw because as yet they don't have a work space. While Ostaszewska and Konarska are in Warsaw, Jankiewicz works from Tel Aviv, and joined us via Skype. Indeed, it is this unusual situation and their nomadic lifestyle that keeps the trio's approach very fresh and open to other experiences. This also has an impact on the way they work and the studio's ambitions, as they are not bound by a set of rules to do with a specific place or project. 'We each have a day job as well,' says Jankiewicz. 'The projects we do with Baba Akcja is what we really want to do. Baba is an extra, but it's very important to us, as it's a way of expressing ourselves.'

Ostaszewska, Konarska and Jankiewicz all graduated from the Academy of Fine Arts in Warsaw in 2006. It wasn't until their final year that they hit it off and thought to do something beyond their college work. So in 2005, they established Baba Akcja. Two weeks after graduation,

Zofia Konarska

Monika Ostaszewska

Discovering Women in Polish Design — **MONIKA OSTASZEWSKA** + **ZOFIA KONARSKA** + **KLEMENTYNA JANKIEWICZ**

Jankiewicz left to carry on her studies for another year at the Bezalel Academy in Jerusalem, and then moved to Tel Aviv. They haven't been altogether in one place since. But this hasn't had an adverse effect on the practice to produce work and initiate projects: the three communicate ideas, discuss details and practice design through Skype and over emails. 'Each one of us looks after a particular aspect of a project,' explains Ostaszewska. 'One develops the packaging, while another puts together the graphics, and then we check everything at the airport before going to a fair or an exhibition. We've been making prototypes in our own homes and using the facilities at the Academy of Fine Arts in Warsaw.'

By selling its products through online shops such as Designboom, Baba Akcja retains a certain amount of control over production and distribution, and by-passes the issues that other Polish designers suffer in a country where communication between manufacturers and designers is limited. Although, this is only a temporary solution. 'We have started to talk to manufacturers in Poland and Israel,' says Jankiewicz. 'We are trying to push for some of our projects to be mass-produced, but it's a long process. Recently, though, people have started to pay attention to our work.'

During our conversation, Ostaszewska and Konarska have been extracting samples of their work from what seems to be a bottomless bag, and within minutes the table has turned into a pop-up studio. The display of colourful objects reflects the vitality and wit underlying Baba Akcja. Most of its projects make some reference to women, for example, Babki, a set of three different-sized sand moulds in the shape of a female breast. 'This was a quick project we did in the summer of 2008 for Gdynia Design Days in Gdańsk. It was fun, but also made a comment about women who want a perfect body,' says Ostaszewska. 'Maybe if the Babka reaches production, we will have to downsize them,' adds Konarska. 'But for the exhibition it was good to have them in exaggerated sizes. It was a funny sight to see everyone playing with them!'

Baba Akcja's latest design is the Sophia Lamp, which is the studio's first project to be sold in shops in Poland as well as online. It consists of a ceramic base and a perforated shade that doubles as an earring display. 'Although this project also directly addresses women, we chose a neutral form so as not to make it exclusive,' says Ostaszewska. Though the designers are keen to see their work mass-produced, they feel very close to the arts, partly due to their education at the Academy in Warsaw. 'The artistic component is very important to us,' explains Jankiewicz. 'Part of our studies was to explore sculpture and fine arts. Sculpture in particular had a strong influence on my approach to design.' In some respects this makes the Polish education system broader in comparison to other European countries, but the distinct lack of aligning education with industry, there is nothing in place to facilitate internships, for example, means that students don't get an opportunity to understand design as a profession.

The popular alternative, however, is the Erasmus programme, which enabled Konarska to study in Portugal and Ostaszewska to study in Ireland for a year. 'My experience in Portugal was a real eye-opener,' says Konarska enthusiastically. 'I focused on graphic design as this was an area my studies at the Academy in Warsaw didn't cover. It was also great to meet designers from other countries and exchange our perspectives and experiences. Some people didn't know Polish design even existed.'

'Well I can see things are changing really fast in Poland,' says Jankiewicz. 'Polish design is making a place for itself, and things are definitely evolving very quickly. It is a great time for designers in Poland, full of possibilities. Similarly, opportunities are everywhere in Israel: everything needs to be designed here.'

It is Ostaszewska who has the last word, and it is something that has been echoed by many of the designers and professionals I have met in Poland. 'I recently visited a friend in Copenhagen, who told me how difficult she has found it as a designer in Denmark, because over there design is integrated into their culture and their commerce,' she says. 'Here in Poland, as is the case in Israel too, it might be hard for us to make a living as designers now, but we have many more opportunities to make a substantial change in Polish design.'

ESSAY
Anna Frąckiewicz on Wanda Telakowska

) **Wanda Telakowska was a remarkable** Polish woman, who, in 1950, initiated the Institute of Industrial Design in Warsaw (Instytut Wzornictwa Przemysłowego: IWP). Telakowska conceived it as a state facility with studios where designers could make prototypes and samples for the industry, as well as conduct academic research. In this respect, the IWP can be viewed as the first school of design in Poland. For some years it also produced its own designs: ceramics, printed textiles, and even furniture, which was made on the premises. The Institute's showroom became a resource of designs, models and prototypes.

Telakowska's vision for Polish design was to create a collaboration between professional and non-professional artists: folk artists, talented people without formal arts education, and children. She believed that such collaboration could create contemporary design that was rooted in local traditions.

Born in 1905 in Sosnowiec, Silesia, Telakowska moved to Warsaw with her family, where her father worked as a construction engineer. She studied painting and graphic arts at the Academy of Fine Arts in Warsaw. Like most of her peers, she also studied pedagogy, and taught drawing at secondary schools.

In the 1930s Telakowska was a successful graphic artist. She took part in several important international exhibitions, and won awards for her work. In 1938 she was employed by the Ministry of Education as an inspector of the vocational (trade) schools, where mostly crafts were taught. This consolidated her interest in education to develop people's creativity, and in shaping their aesthetic sense.

During the Second World War, she taught lettering and advertising in the Secondary School of Commerce. After the war she gave up her artistic career and started to promote Polish design. She even introduced the Polish word for designing, projektowanie, into common parlance. Telakowska was obsessed with the idea that domestic products should be designed by artists, and be both functional and beautiful. Her ambition is characterised by the phrase: beauty everyday, for everyone.

In 1945 she was employed by the Ministry of Culture to organise and run a small division – first named the Department of Planning; the Department of Manufacturing, and finally the Bureau of Supervision of the Production Aesthetic – which aimed to provide prototype designs for light industry, and create a situation in which artistic designs would be mass-produced. To achieve this, Telakowska, between other activities, ordered and bought samples for manufacturers. These craft products included furniture, patterns for printed fabrics, glass, ceramics, toys, souvenirs, metal objects, jewellery, clothes, and fashion accessories. Many of these were considered for mass production, but remained as one-offs because the industry was not interested in new designs. They weren't deemed necessary because in the so-called socialist economy, demand was much greater than supply.

During that time, many artists were inspired by Telakowska and became involved in applied arts. Though craftsmanship was blossoming, it was also the beginning of design as a new branch of visual arts. The artists collaborating with Telakowska came from very different groups, including architects; painters; graduates of Cracow and Warsaw fine arts academies; members of the art collective Ład Cooperative, and also students.

Telakowska was such an independent spirit, and for this reason she was under constant political pressure. Even when her ideas were in accordance with the official party ideology, the authorities considered her as a threat. This fear stemmed from Telakowska's strength of conviction that design was the most democratic way of spreading beauty, and making a more competitive economy. On the other hand, her activities were used as a kind of smokescreen for the authorities (against her wishes), and products from the IWP were showcased at international exhibitions to demonstrate the success and high standard of living in the People's Republic of Poland. In reality, these objects were often only made for the event, and remained inaccessible to the public.

Things didn't improve: during the early 1960s there was an increasing tendency to separate product and industrial design from interior architecture and furniture design. Telakowska was seen as conservative and an obstacle to progress. The younger generation didn't understand her fascination with folk art and her ideas of collaboration with laymen. They believed there was no place for non-professionals in design. The younger generation wanted to be modern and open to the western world and for them, folk art was associated with Socialist Realism and conservative tendencies.

In 1979, when Telakowska was going to retire, she organised for the prototypes and models from the IWP 's showroom and archives, to be handed over to the National Museum in Warsaw. She was afraid that without her presence,

nobody at the IWP would take care of the collection, and it would be destroyed. Although the IWP was never intended to be a museum or gallery, the artefacts from the 1940s formed the collection that became the foundation stone of the Centre of Modern Design, established in 1979.

In 1976 she wrote to a friend explaining the difficulty of coming up against such fierce opposition to her efforts and utopian vision that design could be a tool for shaping culture, even expressing very human concern that she had sacrificed more than herself, but the chance of a family also. Telakowska died 15 January 1985.

In my opinion, Telakowska's vision was to communicate Polish design to as many people as possible. Her ambition was to open people's eyes to beauty, and be able to distinguish between beauty, harmony, and ugliness, and eventually make them need and demand such beauty in everyday things. Despite her efforts to awaken people's creativity and encourage a universal sense of aesthetic in Polish society, she didn't succeed. But thanks to her the IWP came into being along with several great works, now called the icons of Polish design.

She valued teaching and believed this was the key to communicating design to a wide audience, a gift she herself possessed. [Piotr Gołuński, Wanda Telakowska, Dramat demiurga, Projekt 1986 nr 5 / Piotr Gołuński, Wanda Telakowska, Tragedy of the demiurge, Projekt 1986 nr 5, English translation Joanna Holzman]. Artist and designer,

Piotr Gołuński wrote: 'what did she feel when, at the close of her life, she watched, with declined eyes, (as eventually she turned blind) the disintegration of the structures she had so painstakingly built, the gradual decline of her beloved discipline, industrial design, back to the point of departure, the bureaucratization of the institution she had launched, but especially the sinking of the country into a state reminiscent of 1945, when quantity was superior to quality, and mass over the visual value, when it was felt that efforts should again be made to rebuild native culture?'

Telakowska's charm and sense of humour were famous. She had the wonderful ability to laugh at herself and had many friends. It has been said that she easily fell in love, though she was alone all of her life. Besides the legacy of the collection of Polish design, Telakowska also acquired an album of autographs and inscriptions from artists, writers and politicians. The renowned book of notes, commentaries, poems, drawings and jokes serve as a personal portrait of an impressive and extraordinary woman.

ESSAY
Anna Maga on Hanna Chwierut-Jasicka

⟩ Before Wanda Telakowska retired, her last great achievement was to secure the works collected at the design office of the Industrial Design Institute [Instytutu Wzornictwa Przemyslowego: IWP] and those which had been gathered during the period before the activities of the Institute.

She identified herself with this project, and there is no doubt that this was her oeuvre. Anxious about the future of the collection, which had already gained a value worthy of museum presentation, Telakowska was systematic in her work. In 1973 she invited Hanna Chwierut-Jasicka to IWP. Chwierut-Jasicka was an art historian and museologist, who had worked at the State Ethnographic Museum and the Mechanical Documentation Archives in Poland. Her task was to systematise and perform an initial analysis of the collection.

Chwierut-Jasicka had also previously worked at the Studio of Local Artistic Inventions in Industrial Design of the IWP for five years, and could use her knowledge of folk art to work on the non-professional artefacts in the collection. She also had a broad view of contemporary art, including the value of applied art and design, and understood the complexity of Polish design of the time. When she accepted the position as curator of the design collection, which had been transferred by the IWP to the National Museum in Warsaw, she wanted to document both the history, as well as contemporary achievements of this field of fine arts.

In 1979, a new department was opened at the National Museum: the Centre of Modern Design [Ośrodek Wzornictwa Nowoczesnego]. This could not have happened without the support of high ministerial officers, and was made possible by the director of the Museum at the time, Stanisław Lorentz. Although old art was closer to the professor's heart, he was nonetheless ready to open up to a new field.

There were many of those who opposed the idea of this new department of the Museum. For many years the collection was not fully appreciated and although the art of design defended its position as being a natural consequence of the evolution of handicraft, many art historians found it difficult to accept that works of art such as paintings and sculptures were under one roof with mass-produced objects of applied art. But Chwierut-Jasicka was convinced that the decision was right and devoted the last 15 years of her life to the collection and the Centre, which became a meeting place for researchers and designers, representing different thoughts and circles.

Chwierut-Jasicka had a clearly defined idea of how to further develop the project. In The Design Collection at the National Museum in Warsaw [Zbiory wzornictwa w Muzeum Narodowym w Warszawie] 1986, Chwierut-Jasicka wrote in an IWP bulletin publication, Design – the news of the Institute of Industrial Design: 'when taking over the collection we were aware of how fragmented it was – both in terms of reflecting the design works carried out at the Institute, as well as in terms of the actual image of Polish design. We have, therefore, defined the following tasks in building the programme of the further collection of the material documentation of Polish design as an artistic discipline: completing the histories of the collection, shifting the scope of interest of our institution further back in history; expanding the collection to include the design works by authors from the IWP; enriching our collection by valuable examples of design created in other institutions, universities, industry, [and] acquiring material products of different areas of life related to design.

'We have also decided to develop appropriate criteria of developing such collections, which by means of their diversity would create a real reflection of contemporary culture in its entirety and, in line with the mission of the National Museum, would represent artistic values, as well as constitute a material which would be valuable to researchers, and representatives when exhibited.

'Being aware of the dangers entailed in excessive collecting, which jeopardises the appropriate means of preserving collected works, as well as taking into consideration the need to provide proper conservatory care and full scientific attention... we have to limit ourselves to securing only the selected works of utmost significance. Hence, it is just as important as collecting to be in constant touch with design studios, i.e. places where the collections are created, and to provide these studios with support in their proper organisation and development of content, and – should the situation of the collection be in any way threatened – to acquire the most valuable objects....

'These criteria are as follows: 1) collecting items designed by a given author, a professional designer with an education in fine arts, successfully presenting his/her works at exhibitions domestically and abroad, consciously aiming at achieving his/her artistic goals, providing a creative contribution to the cooperation with a technologist or constructor, which can be defined in the convention of the design as a contemporarily understood artistic discipline; 2) an opinion about the value of the object confirmed by an award or by mentions in publications; many of the objects accepted to the collection are accompanied by recommendations of artists or theoreticians, widely respected in the area of applied design; 3) a set of features distinguishing a given work for reason of its impact in the creative field, specific characteristics typical of a good design which are common in the work of many artists creating in the same material or genre.

'In order to explain the creation of museum collections of industrial design, it would be best to present examples of the collection at exhibitions... we have organised.'

Despite such a precisely determined system of criteria, Chwierut-Jasicka's broad view as a person managing the department is extremely positive. I also applaud the fact that she didn't always adhere to these rigorous criteria. It is often difficult to assess 'fresh' objects met for the first time, and it's easy to make a mistake and rashly reject projects which have not yet been 'tested'.

At the beginning, Chwierut-Jasicka only had one assistant and one laboratory worker to do the tedious job of organising the collected works and create an inventory. As there was no possibility of getting an exhibition space, Chwierut-Jasicka's intention was to arrange the storage space to make it accessible to small groups of visitors from all backgrounds. In terms of the science of museology, this was wrong. However, from the point of view of the mission that Chwierut-Jasicka undertook: collecting good Polish design and developing it, this solution was necessary.

The development of the collection depended as much on her contacts with contemporary designers, as with the industry. The aim was to expand the collection through donations from authors and producers, and by supporting designers in the industry or supporting the industry by promoting creative designers. Needless to say, these relationships were not always idyllic, however they often bore fruit, and confirmed us all in the sense of our work.

Chwieruta-Jasicka had a strong personality. She was very demanding of her associates. These traits gave her the strength and power to push through many actions, so that our centre could develop and its esteem could grow, despite the unfavourable circumstances. I took over

from Chwierut-Jasicka in 1994, and have since then been manager of the Centre. Unfortunately, these unfavourable conditions, particularly the premises, are still valid. The mission of developing the collection requires a lot of perseverance. We can no longer do what Chwierut-Jasicka did in the 1980s, and provide access to the 'open' storage, as they have been filled over 30 years, and any presentation is impossible without dedicted space.

The Centre collects Polish designers' works. From the moment of its inception, the collection has been systematically filled with contemporary pieces, both unique, and mass-produced, as well as work from the period between the two world wars. The collection hosts over 24,000 objects spanning a vast range of products and material. The Centre has organised and co-organised 19 exhibitions. The most important ones include: Polish Design in the 40 years of the Polish People's Republic, 1984; The Ouvre of Wanda Zawidzka-Manteuffel, 1994; ŁAD Artists' Cooperative: 1926-1996 in 1996; Common Wealth, Polish Products 1899-1999, in 2000, and What Toys! [Ale zabawki], 2008.

Chwieruta-Jasicka has created a team of associates who are engaged and loyal to its institution. The work she started is carried forward by three Annas: Demska, Frąckiewicz, and Maga. She has infected us all with her perseverance, stemming from the deep faith of the righteous cause of the mission to develop design; scientifically organise the collections; prepare exhibitions; give back to our culture the forgotten works of Polish design, and popularise the achievements of contemporary authors.

Work & Biographies ⟩

Work & Biographies
Designers

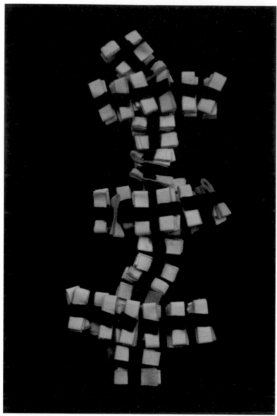

Textile, hand-stitched silk. **2008**

Magdalena Komar
Textile designer

Komar trained as a textile designer at the Ecole Supérieure des Artes et Technique de la Mode (Esmod) in Paris and studied multimedia textiles at Loughborough University in the UK. Subsequently, she established her own fashion brand Magalena, designing and producing haute couture textile accessories. Komar is represented by the textile agent Julius Schofield from Indesign.
www.magalena.com

Maja Ganszyniec
Product designer

Ganszyniec graduated in interior architecture at the Academy of Fine Arts in Cracow in 2005. She completed her MA in design products at the Royal College of Art in London In 2008. Ganszyniec's work received the Helen Hamlyn Design Award for Creativity. Ganszyniec works as a freelance designer in Warsaw.
www.majagan.com

6 Degrees, flexible shelving system. **2008**

Dealing with Consumption –
Polish design exhibition for St-Étienne Biennale. **2004**

Marta Białecka + Anna Piwowar
Product and graphic designers

Białecka and Piwowar met at the Academy of Fine Arts in Warsaw and established La Polka in 2005. Since then, they have taken part in exhibitions in Poland and abroad. They work in the field of graphic, industrial and interior design. They have recently collaborated with artists Dorota Kozieradzka and Michał Szuszkiewicz in a scenography project for the Centre for Contemporary Art Ujazdowski Castle in Warsaw.
www.lapolka.com

Dog-Trick lamp. **2007**

Ewa Gołębiowska
Director of The Silesian Castle of Art and Enterprise

Gołębiowska graduated from Jagielloński University in Polish philology. In 1992 she became a director of the faculty of Education, Culture, Tourism and Sport in the Town Hall of Cieszyn. Since 2005 she has worked as director of The Silesian Castle of Art and Enterprise in Cieszyn, the only regional design centre in Poland. From 2005 to 2007 she coordinated the Silesian Design Network.
www.zamekcieszyn.pl

Anna Łoskiewicz + Zofia Strumiłło-Sukiennik
Product designers

Łoskiewicz and Strumiłło-Sukiennik graduated from the Faculty of Industrial Design, Academy of Fine Arts in Warsaw in 2003. In the same year they founded Beza Projekt, which is interested in functionality with a tongue-in-cheek approach. The studio has exhibited its work in many design fairs such as IMM Cologne, Messe Frankfurt, and the Łódź Design Festival.
www.bezaprojekt.pl

Play & Joke exhibition, Łódź Design Festival. **2008**

Nail Table. **2006**

Agnieszka Jacobson-Cielecka
Journalist and curator

Jacobson-Cielecka trained at the Academy of Fine Arts in Gdańsk. She was the founding editor of the Polish Elle Decoration and the Prodeco design awards, Jacobson-Cielecka was the curator and art director of the Łódź Design Festival in 2008 and 2009. She is the representative of the Vitra Design Museum in Poland and is a freelance consultant for interiors and design brands.
www.lodzdesign.com

Magdalena Lubińska
Founder of Moho Design

Lubińska studied law at the Silesian University in Katowice. In 2004 she founded Moho Design, the rug and carpet company, which combines new production technologies with craft. In 2006 Moho Design was awarded by Wallpaper with the Design Award in the Best Textile category for its _mohohej!DIA rug. In 2008 the company received the Red Dot Product Design, and Design Management Europe Award as New Comers.
www.mohodesign.com

Photo — Michal Korta

Comma Chair, Noti. 2007

The Natural Rock Collection, rug. **2007**

Renata Kalarus
Product designer

Kalarus graduated in industrial design at the Academy of Arts in Cracow. She was awarded the Perfect Thing 2000 prize for her Kiwi sofa and Chair 94. In 2007 she received the Prodeco award 2006 for a functionally diverse collection of sofas called Bibik Loft. Kalarus' Comma Chair received an honorable mention for Product Design at Red Dot 2009.
www.kalarus.com

The Time is Now, part of Future Design – Time for Relax exhibition. **2008**

Beata Bochińska
President of the Board, Institute of Industrial Design in Warsaw

Art historian and design critic, Bochińska holds an MA from the University of Warsaw. Since 2006 she has worked for the Ministry of Economy managing the Institute of Industrial Design (Instytut Wzornictwa Przemysłowego), the leading industrial design company in Poland, established and owned by the Polish government, one of the first such entities in post-war Europe.
www.iwp.com.pl

Anna Kotowicz-Puszkarewicz
Product designer

Kotowicz-Puszkarewicz graduated in history of art from the Cardinal Stefan Wyszyński University in Warsaw in 2002 and in graphic design from the Academy of Fine Arts in Łódź in 2005. Together with Artur Puszkarewicz in 2006, she established Aze design, a design practice specialising in product and graphic design. Aze design showed work in Play & Joke, as part of the Łódź Design Festival in 2008.
www.azedesign.pl

Tense coat hanger. **2008**

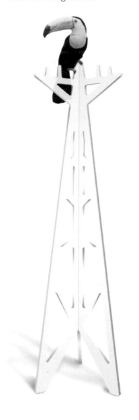

360° Trend Report books, Red Dot for Communication. **2009**

Ela Skrzypek + **Magda Małczyńska-Umeda**
Designers

Skrzypek and Małczyńska-Umeda both graduated in
graphic design from the Academy of Fine Arts in Warsaw
in 1999 and established Bakalie in 2000. Skrzypek,
creative director and partner, was awarded the British
Council's International Young Design Entrepreneur of
the Year 2005 prize at 100% Design in London. Skrzypek
is among the founding members of the Polish Graphic
Designers Association.
www.studiobakalie.pl

Poczta Polska, postage stamps. **2005**

Zuzanna Skalska
Senior consultant in design trends and insights

Skalska studied at the Design Academy Eindhoven and
Royal Academy of Fine Art in Den Bosch. Since 2001
Skalska has worked as a trend watcher for VanBerlo
Strategy + Design, her research provides the basis for the
360° Trend Report books which was awarded the Red Dot
2009 for Communication. She is a member of the board
of Dutch Design Week and assistant professor at the
University Eindhoven, department of Industrial Design.
www.linkedin.com/in/zuzanna

Agata Kulik-Pomorska
Product designer

In 2005 Kulik-Pomorska set up Malafor with Paweł
Pomorski. In 2006 it participated in Inspired by Cologne
Young Talents Show at IMM Cologne in Germany. In 2008
Malafor exhibited at the Polish Institute in Budapest,
Hungary. In the same year they participated in the Łódź
Design Festival.
www.malafor.com

Second Life Series & Rest, stool. **2009**

Dismantable Ball, prototype for a toy. **1975**

Teresa Kruszewska
Interior designer

Kruszewska studied interior design at the Academy of
Fine Arts in Warsaw and graduated in 1951. Since then,
Kruszewska has been a freelance designer specialising
in children's furniture and, up until 1978 she taught at
the Department of Interior Design at the Academy of
Fine Arts in Warsaw. Kruszewska's work is part of the
main collection of the National Museum in Warsaw and
Poznań; in the Rhode Island School of Design, and the
Vitra Design Museum in Germany.

Anna Wojczyńska
Interior designer

In 1989 Wojczyńska founded the interior design studio
Vis à Vis with Wojciech Wachowski. In 1996 they founded
Zoom showroom and gallery, and in 2007 the eponymous
online shop to promote Polish design. Wojczyńska writes
about contemporary design in magazines such as Futu
and Gazeta Wyborcza.
www.visavis.com.pl
www.zoomzoom.pl

Tam Tam washbasin for Logo. **1999**

6OBAG (designed with Remigiusz Truchanowicz),
biodegradable carrier bag. **2008**

Katarzyna Okińczyc
Product designer

Katarzyna Okińczyc graduated in industrial design and
architecture at the Academy of Fine Arts in Poznań in
2001. She then studied industrial design at Masters level
at the Berlin University of the Arts in 2004. Okińczyc
worked in Boston for design consultancy Eleven, and
Christopher Streng Design studio in Chicago, before
setting up as a freelance designer in Warsaw.
www.okinczyc.com

XXL, inflatable chandelier. **2009**

Anna Siedlecka
Product designer and lighting manufacturer

Siedlecka studied interior architecture and design
at the Academy of Fine Arts in Gdańsk. In 2004 she
founded Puff-Buff design studio with architect Radek
Achramowicz, working on interior and product design
projects. In 2006 the studio started to design
and manufacture decorative lighting. In 2009 it launched
its latest light Orca at Euroluce and Zona Tortona in
Milan, Italy.
www.puff-buff.com

Marta Rowińska
Designer

Rowińska graduated in architecture in 2001 from the
University of Warsaw and in textile and fashion from the
Łódź Academy of Fine Arts in 2006. In 2007, with Lech
Rowiński, she established the design studio Beton and
collaborated with choreographer and artist Rodney Place
as a costume designer for his Angels of Stealth dance
performance series. In 2008 Rowińska participated to
the Łódź Design Festival.
www.beton-on.com

Fi/2 bag in polyethylene foam. **2007**

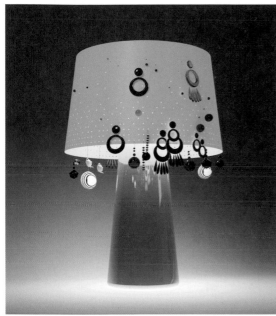

Sophia Lamp and storage. **2008**

**Monika Ostaszewska + Zofia Konarska +
Klementyna Jankiewicz**
Product designers

The team behind Baba Akcja graduated together in 2005
at the industrial design department of the Academy of
Fine Arts in Warsaw and established the studio in the
same year. In 2007 they participated in 100% Design
Tokyo. In 2008 Baba Akcja participated in the Future
Design exhibition with the Relax Instant project. Baba
Akcja's products are mostly available online from
Designboom and MagazynPraga.
www.babaakcja.com

Biographies
Authors

Gian Luca Amadei

⟩ Gian Luca Amadei is a freelance journalist and writer.
Trained as an interior designer at the University for the Creative Arts where he graduated in 2005, Amadei subsequently took an MSc in Architecture History, under Professor Adrian Forty at the the Bartlett in London. Since April 2007 he has been the product editor for Blueprint magazine. Amadei has also taught at the the School of the Built Environment at Nottingham University and at the University for the Creative Arts. His interest in photography has led to commissions for Italian furniture companies, such as Moroso and Schiffini, and for London-based architecture practices. As well as writing, Amadei is currently working on a PhD in architecture at the University of Kent.

Vicky Richardson

⟩ Vicky Richardson is an architectural writer and editor.
Since 2004 she has been editor of Blueprint magazine. She regularly chairs architecture and design events, and has been a jury member for many high-profile design competitions. Richardson is a member of the London Mayor's Cultural Strategy Group and a trustee of the educational charity, The Campaign for Drawing. She studied fine art at Chelsea School of Art before taking an architecture degree. However, she never became an architect, instead choosing to write about the subject, first as deputy editor on the RIBA Journal, and later as a freelance writer. She has written several books, including In Defence of the Dome (1999) and New Vernacular Architecture (2002).

Czesława Frejlich

⟩ Czesława Frejlich has an MA and PhD from the Industrial Design Department, Academy of Fine Arts in Cracow (1975) where she also holds a post as a professor. In 2000 she started teaching at the Industrial Design Department, Academy of Fine Arts in Warsaw. Since 2001 editor-in-chief of the Polish Design Quarterly 2+3D, Frejlich has also curated major design shows such as Common Wealth (Warsaw and Kraków 2000; Poznań 2001); Dealing with Consumption (St-Étienne, 2004), and Real-World Laboratory – Design from Central Europe (St-Étienne, 2008). Among her many publications about design, in 2001 Frejlich published Common Wealth, a comprehensive book on Polish products between 1899-1999.

Anna Maga

⟩ Anna Maga is an art historian. She received her diploma at the University of Warsaw in 1981. Since 1993, she has been curator of the Centre of Modern Design at the National Museum in Warsaw, where she started working in 1981. Interested in the history of Polish design – especially furniture and glass – she has curated many exhibitions, the most important of which are: The Ład Artists Cooperative 1926-1996; Common Wealth; Polish Products 1899-1999, and Toys. She has also written about Polish design, including the book, Common Wealth in 2001.

Anna Frąckiewicz

) **Anna Frąckiewicz graduated in art history in 1992**
from the Institute of Art History at the University of
Warsaw. In the same year, before graduation, she
started working at the Warsaw National Museum's
Centre of Modern Design. In 1995, Frąckiewicz
spent one month in the UK, as part of a scholarship
organised by the British Council, and worked with
Lou Taylor from the University of Brighton and
David Crowley from the Victoria and Albert Museum
in London.

In the late Nineties, Frąckiewicz researched the history
and output of Polish art collective Ład Cooperative,
and produced the monograph, Spółdzielnia Artystów
Ład 1926-1996, and an exhibition in 1997 at the
Academy of Fine Arts in Warsaw, and later at the
Central Textile Museum in Łódź. Frąckiewicz's studies
range from Polish architects from the Twenties and
Thirties in relation to their furniture and interior
design production, to Polish art deco, and 1950s
Socialist Realist interior architecture, applied
and decorative arts. Her ongoing project explores
the documentation of the collection of porcelain
figurines designed and made at the Institute of
Industrial Design between 1956-1964.

Dario Lombardi

) **Dario Lombardi was born in Rome, Italy. In 1996 he**
completed his Master of Photography, at the Istituto
Superiore di Fotografia e Comunicazione Integrata,
in Rome. He now lives and works as a freelance
photographer in Vienna, Austria. Lombardi has
always worked in portrait photography, starting
with theatre and dance developing a passion for
fashion photography. His latest project Hinsichtlich-
Regarding, tells a story of Persian women wearing
and sharing their lives with the veil.

Anna Pietrzyk-Simone

) **Anna Pietrzyk–Simone received an MA in**
management from the University of Warsaw in 2000.
Between 2000 and 2004, Pietrzyk–Simone was
based in South Africa, working for Interactive Africa
on projects that aimed to advertise Cape Town as the
creative capital of the Republic and develop creative
industries through the Design Indaba brand.

Since 2004, she has worked as head of communications
for Ross Lovegrove, as well as consultant for
leading Polish design brands such as Moho Design,
representing them abroad as well as facilitating
collaborations between Polish companies and
foreign designers. Pietrzyk-Simone is co-curator and
producer of the Young Creative Poland exhibition
which is part of POLSKA! YEAR 2009-2010, the
UK cultural programme coordinated by the Adam
Mickiewicz Institute. The exhibition will take place
during the London Design Festival 2009.

Credits ⟩

A YEAR OF CONTEMPORARY EVERYTHING FROM POLSKA! 2009—2010 POLSKAYEAR.PL

—

FILM, THEATRE, LITERATURE, ARCHITECTURE, ART, DESIGN, MUSIC, FASHION

Patron HM The Queen
Patron HE The President
of the Republic of Poland

Adam Mickiewicz Institute

) **POLSKA! YEAR is the official name of a**
cultural project promoting Poland in
the UK. It comprises over 200 projects
introducing the most interesting
achievements of Polish culture and
works of the most outstanding Polish
artists to the British public. The
programme includes extraordinary
exhibits from Polish museum collections
and works of young contemporary
artists and designers, concerts with
Polish performers, as well as Polish
music performed by British bands and
soloists. There are theatrical and dance
performances, reviews of Polish dramatic
productions and events promoting Polish
literature at selected literary festivals.

POLSKA! YEAR presents a vast cultural
programme which would not have been
possible without strict cooperation
with British partners i.e. key cultural
institutions: museums, galleries, festivals,
theatres, concert halls and many others.

POLSKA! YEAR is coordinated by the Adam
Mickiewicz Institute, a government
organization responsible for the
promotion of Polish culture abroad.
POLSKA! YEAR in the UK 2009-2010
takes place under the patronage of HM
The Queen and HE The President of the
Republic of Poland.

DuPont™ Corian®

) Officially launched on the US market in 1967, DuPont™ Corian® was developed by a team of DuPont scientists in the early Sixties within a broader research programme. The company established a division called Building Products Venture in order to develop different materials, technologies and products for interior design (kitchen, bathroom, furnishing) and architecture. The team behind DuPont™ Corian® wanted to create a versatile, easily formable and hygienic composite material combining high-quality properties and performance of selected minerals and man-made resins. The result, a few decades later, was a material that solved a wide variety of functional and aesthetic needs, one that has become an icon for both industry and creative minds.

During the Seventies and Eighties, DuPont™ Corian® became increasingly commercialized and, since the early Nineties, it has been incorporated in most of the interior design applications in both commercial and residential environments around the world.

In the late Nineties, DuPont took a major step forward and significantly strengthened its dialogue with the community of professionals in architecture and design worldwide. A milestone in this process came in 2000 when the company collaborated with Italian design and architecture practice Sottsass Associati, headed by Ettore Sottsass, one of the most important figures in modern design.

DuPont™ Corian® began collaborating with cutting-edge kitchen, bathroom, furniture and design companies, such as Cappellini, Boffi, B&B Italia, Established & Sons, and with architects and designers such as Ingo Maurer, Jean Nouvel, Marc Newson, Ronan and Erwan Bouroullec, and Ron Arad, to mention just a few.

It is worth mentioning some of the most significant projects, including Z Island by DuPont™ Corian® a high-tech, futuristic kitchen designed by Zaha Hadid and launched at Milan Design Week 2006. In Milan the following year, the innovative Corian® Nouvel Lumieres interior was conceived by Jean Nouvel. In 2008 the colourful Corian® loves MISSONI project by Rosita and Luca Missoni, combined design excellence with the genial creativity and style of Missoni fashion brand. And in 2008, the unique and astonishing outdoor installation, The Gavin Jones Garden of Corian® was created by Philip Nash for the Chelsea Flower Show in London.

Its latest project, CORIAN® super-surfaces, designed by Amanda Levete Architects, created a challenging new shaping technique, which enables DuPont™ Corian® to be used as a structural material.

DuPont™ Corian® is relatively new to the scene, considering that marble, granite, stone, glass and wood have a history spanning thousands of years. DuPont™ Corian® is developing fast, however, and is continuously entering new areas of applications, thanks to the technical and scientific know-how of DuPont and the relationship it has built with the most advanced professionals in industry, architecture and design.

Recently, DuPont undertook an enormous architecture project in Africa's Ivory Coast, where DuPont™ Corian® has been used as external cladding covering 8,000sq m of a large congress centre, due to reach completion in September 2009. The Palais des Congrès' panels will feature a complex, three-dimensional pattern (reproducing the relief motif of the original ceramic tile facade) applied using advanced computer-controlled and moulding machines.

The company is also collaborating with Zehnder Group to bring a groundbreaking collection of radiators in DuPont™ Corian®, which will hit the market in late 2009.

DuPont prides itself on being at the forefront of design development and championing design communities worldwide. In 2008, DuPont™ Corian® supported the Łódź Design Festival in Poland, which opened up new opportunities for collaborations in the Polish design and art scene.

Since which time, DuPont has helped many Polish designers and artists aiming to develop a bigger and stronger design community in Poland by reinforcing a critical link with local manufacturers and suppliers. Recently, DuPont collaborated with renowned Polish designer Tomek Rygalik, who designed a new lighting installation using DuPont™ Corian®. The project was unveiled in June 2009, as one of the key events at Poznań's Arena Design, the leading interior design fair in Poland. Rygalik's installation was presented in an old meat factory, the raw ex-industrial spaces, well contrasted Rygalik's delicate and unique creations.

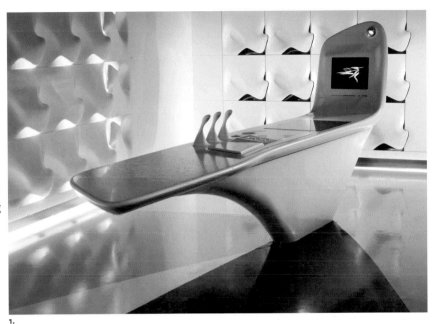
1.

2.

1. Z Island by DuPont™ Corian® kitchen project, design Zaha Hadid for DuPont™ Corian® event at 2007 Milan week of design, photo Leo Torri for DuPont™ Corian®, all rights reserved

2. Table Tree centerpiece in DuPont™ Corian®, design Matali Crasset for Corian®: 40 Years – 40 designers exhibition; photo Leo Torri for DuPont™ Corian®, all rights reserved

Domo

) **One of the main ambitions of Domo**
television is to promote Polish design,
which has recently established itself
on the world design stage. From the
offset, Domo television cooperated with
the award-winning Moho design studio
run by Magda Lubińska and Michał
Biernacki. This resulted in creating
woolen gadgets made of woven cloth,
the same fabric that was used for
the multi award-winning _mohohej!DIA
rug by Moho Design.

The documentary, directed by Jacek
Dużyński, consists of 19 comprehensive
stories, based on the original idea of
Italian journalist and writer Gian Luca
Amadei, author of the book Discovering
Women in Polish Design: Interviews &
Conversations. What really inspired the
producer to make this documentary
was the remarkable number of female
designers that Poland boasts compared
to other countries. The documentary
demonstrates the importance and
subsequent emergence of women in
the industry. Designers present their
work and achievements, so that the
audience can form their own opinions.
There are also a number of interviews
with established female designers who
have a great respect for the environment.
It is the producer's belief that within a
few years Poland will gain international
recognition for its designers.

Meeting female designers and getting to
understand the design world was inspiring
for the film's creators. They were surprised
by the fact that it is so industrious and
highly sophisticated. While making the
film, the team visited many design studios
in various regions of Poland. In each
place they were met with a wonderful
and friendly atmosphere. Despite the
cameras, protagonists were natural and
very pleased to talk about their work,
which is also their passion. The film was
ordered by Domo television in 2009.
Director: Jacek Dużyński
Production manager: Anna Sowa

Domo is the first and only Polish digital
TV channel specialising in all aspects
of home design, covering subjects
such as architecture, decorating, DIY,
landscaping and the environment.
Taking a modern approach to subjects,
it broadcasts a variety of genres,
including documentaries, reality shows,
lifestyle programmes, but also drama
and comedy series and movies. Domo
is owned and operated by CANAL+
Cyfrowy, part of Groupe CANAL+.

Photo— Anna Pietrzyk-Simone

Blueprint

) Blueprint is delighted to be media partner
for Discovering Women in Polish Design.
With a 25-year track record as the leading
magazine for architecture and design,
Blueprint is regarded by many around the
world as the original design magazine.

Following the magazine's relaunch in
September 2006, it was described by The
Observer newspaper as the 'design bible'.
Blueprint's award-winning design sets it
apart from other magazines. Published
monthly, it is lovingly produced in large
format on the best quality of paper,
with photography and illustration of
the highest standard. Its long-standing
appeal is also due to the finest criticism,
news and feature writing on design and
architecture, directed at professionals
and non-professionals alike.

Blueprint is available from all leading design
and architecture bookshops, and
from selected newsagents. An annual
subscription of 12 issues costs just £46
(UK). For further details and to subscribe
go to www.blueprintmagazine.co.uk or
call +44 (0)834 155 1845

BLUEPRINT
THE LEADING MAGAZINE OF ARCHITECTURE AND DESIGN

JAVIER MARISCAL
JAN DE COCK
ANDY COUNCIL

RON ARAD'S DESIGN MUSEUM IN ISRAEL

PLUS 50 OF THE BEST UK DESIGN GRADUATES

Publisher

Adam Mickiewicz Institute
CULTURE.PL

Sponsors

DOMO

Media Partners

BLUEPRINT

ARCHITEKTURA
murator

Marketing i sprzedaż

orbita

Launch of the book organised
with kind support from

BROMPTON
DESIGN
DISTRICT

THE
LONDON
DESIGN
FESTIVAL